THE REDBECK ANTHOLOGY OF
BRITISH SOUTH ASIAN POETRY

*Dedicated to the first generation of South Asians
who crossed 'the black waters' to settle in Britain*

THE REDBECK ANTHOLOGY OF
BRITISH SOUTH ASIAN POETRY

edited by
Debjani Chatterjee

2000

THE REDBECK ANTHOLOGY OF
BRITISH SOUTH ASIAN POETRY
is published by
Redbeck Press, 24 Aireville Road,
Frizinghall, Bradford, BD9 4HH, UK

ISBN 0 946980 76 4
First published 2000

Cover design based on the painting "Zones of Dreams"
by Salima Hashmi, with kind permission of
Cartwright Hall Art Gallery, Lister Park, Bradford

Design and print by Tony Ward,
Arc & Throstle Press, Shaw Wood Road,
Todmorden, Lancs. OL14 6DA

Redbeck Press acknowledges financial assistance
from Yorkshire Arts Board. It would also like to express
its gratitude to Salt Foundation for its financial assistance.

CONTENTS

FOREWORD

South Asian contribution to British Literature in English has come a long way since the publication of *Travels of Deen Mahomet* (1794) by Sake Deen Mahomed, the first Indian author to publish a book in English. The poets in this anthology are all of South Asian origin. They are first or second generation immigrants from India, Pakistan, Bangladesh and Sri Lanka, or have come from countries in Africa and the Caribbean which experienced substantial migration from India during the years of the Raj.

It has been a privilege to contact South Asian poets all over Britain and to edit this collection for publication in the new Millenium - surely a good time to reflect if South Asian poetry in Britain, like the many award-winning novels by South Asian writers, has finally come of age. The poets here are a very diverse group from many backgrounds and cover a wide age range. The poems too are varied in style and content, although some common themes do surface. These are poets who have many mother tongues, among them: Bengali, Hindi, Urdu, Punjabi, Gujerati, Sinhala, Creole, Swahili, as well as English. Some are distinguished writers in languages other than English and are probably unfamiliar to readers in English. Some are celebrities in non-literary spheres. Some are 'ordinary' people and include students and housewives who count writing poetry in English among their interests. Some are also South Asian writers in English who have established considerable reputations and there are others here who are surely among the literary successes of the coming century.

It has long been my wish to compile an anthology to showcase and celebrate contemporary British South Asian poetry in English. But a few publishers whom I approached felt that, though it was a good idea, they had no funding support to publish it or that 'the time was not yet right'. I wish to record my grateful thanks to David Tipton of Redbeck Press for publishing this anthology and for trusting me to edit it. South Asian poetry in Britain excites me with its versatility and its range, and I find its richness breathtaking. My selection of poems from the many compelling voices that I hear is inevitably a subjective one, but I hope that many will enjoy reading the choices that I have made and that this book will leave a lasting impression.

Debjani Chatterjee, November 1999

DAISY ABEY

ONLY

I live in this derelict house:
stone-built, cracked roof tiles made of village clay
hallmarked from the Red Hills,
mildew conquering the window ledge,
rain water dripping through the kitchen window,
rusty liquid collecting in a tarnished brass pail.
She is frail, her voice trembling,
the old man a skeleton, a century old
like a crumbling rock weathered in rain.
Hot sun, night frost, the prevailing wind exposing
to the sea the erosion of monsoon waves.
He walks with the help of a stick,
she with aluminium crutches,
hand in hand along the avenues,
purple cordylines, poinsettias and bright bougainvillaea.
They sit in the parlour
gazing at the evening sky
filled with the scent of gardenias,
the sun's flickering light a soft grey shade.
Two foot high anthills by the front door steps,
silvery sloughed skins on the dusty doormat.
I heard the hissing sound of a snake, venomous.
I walked up the curved wooden stairs,
windows closed to the daylight,
cobwebs woven into a pattern of wheels,
rotten mangoes, bananas and wild berries in a corner,
covered in black hairy fungus, the bittersweet smell of liquorice
mixed with the excrement of night bats.
A mahogany linen chest on the narrow landing opened,
a discoloured copper key sits in the lock, untouched,
half empty, moth-eaten green silk rags, decades old,
a wall clock with oily patches in Roman numerals;
it is five past one.
Under the satin bed a photograph lies upside down.
She is smiling, holding a bouquet of roses,
white veil draped over her neck and shoulders,
flowing above her golden hair.
His smile majestic.

GHOST GAMES

At night I hear them play in the damp cellars,
they cry, they laugh.
Hush! Hush! Walk on tiptoe,
the long trailing sound of pull-along toys,
up and down the steps, squeaky ducks and
spilling bubble bath, lollipop sticks, paintings of
their grimy hands on white walls, pencil marks;
they disappear behind the doors, windows, cupboards
and lavatories, hide and seek in the store room,
cobwebs on their sticky hair.
They look through the fanlights, keyholes, ring
the door bell, rattling the keys, their shadowy figures
smell of meadow grass.
Knock knock on doors, break the icicles on my
window, open the apple boxes in the loft, drink water
from the tank.
They turn flowerpots upside down, chase each
other down the gravel path. I hear them running
out of the garden gate and hide beneath the
blankets of thick fog.
Their clothes green, blue, yellow, they wear scarlet bonnets.
Hush! Hush!
I hear the goblins play at night.

SHANTA ACHARYA

THE NIGHT OF SHIVA

1

In my top-floor maisonette
solitary in Highgate,
on the eve of *Shiva-Ratri*
in my own way I celebrate
Shiva's commemoration night
reading ancient Hindu folklore;
fasting on a feast of fruits
from foreign shores -
pineapples, pomegranates, plums,
kiwi-fruits, mandarins and dates -
as I chant *Om Namah Shivayam*:
magic formula for the alchemy
of sins into some rare nirvana,
keeping vigil for a god
whose face had etched
itself into my tabernacle
memory as a curious child
one summer afternoon in
the golden time of discovery
in a sprawling bungalow
on the banks of Mahanadi
when the world was revealed
framed in a poster
not of an Indian film-star
but a face to remember,
to love and cherish
though not to obey -
my Lord Shiva.

2

My restless mind wanders back
to a moonless night in Bhubaneswar,
home of gods and city of temples
of exquisite beauty and mosaic history,
where I dissolve like the first rains
of the monsoon into the parched earth.

I remember the night of Shiva
with father in white, crisp dhoti
and tussar punjabi-shirt;
mother in yarns of peacock-
throated pasapali silk changing colour
with the night's chameleon lights:
elephants, lotuses, lions, mandalas,
shielding her from evil eyes,
mantra woven into the Orissi fabric.
My brothers more modern in jeans,
T-shirts, seiko watches, nike shoes.

3

To the temple of Shiva we flocked
like lost sheep in search of our shepherd.
Lingaraja -
shrine dedicated to the face of my dreams,
though worshipped by millions in his *lingam*,
a munificent phallus erect on his Parvati's *yoni*!
Strange indeed are the ways of our gods,
the representation of our perception of IT;
a position unlisted in the *Kama Sutra*.

In all the temples of Shiva tonight,
women will kiss the *lingam* without shame or thought.
Contraception, pills, IUDs, condoms
were unfamiliar verbal territory,
but AIDS or HIV had not yet scarred
our fragile, adolescent memory.

We had not accounted for homosexuality;
I think not, in the midst of such inebriety.
Our childhood was spiced with the *masala* of piety.
Perhaps, I will thank Lord Shiva tonight
for our accidental innocence and simplicity.

4

With the pilgrims from neighbouring villages,
we lit rows of earthen lamps, camphor, incense;
offered coconuts, flowers, silver coins, prayers

for the many miracles to transform our lives!

We waited for the high-priest's communion
as he drew a halo around our heads,
his *arati* blessing us; the rice and the *tulsi*
nestling in the curls of my thick, black hair
as he gave us each the sacred vermilion
on a tender *bel-patri*, green as memory.

Chanting Shiva's name, hundreds of them,
like the thousand-petalled lotus,
he offered us the *diya*, the holy flame,
fresh sandalwood paste for our foreheads
and Ganges water in a bronze chalice.
I preferred to close my eyes, palms folded in prayer
while I felt the sandalwood paste tighten my skin.
Anchored in the middle of a bubbling, vulvic geyser
into whose vortex the priests poured offerings -
coconut, milk, flowers with fragrances of all kinds,
silver and gold snakes bouncing with bananas
gone rusty brown like discarded members afloat -
stood solid in stone, the object of our worship!

Bare-foot in sacred mud, ooze and slime,
we walked like seasoned explorers on a slippery climb,
swaying to the rhythm of the divine temenos
situated in the cave-womb lit with a circle of lamps
of hope and despair, faith and forgiveness.

Blessed and blessing, we finally joined the revellers
cheering the novice clambering to the temple-pinnacle
like the monkey-god Hanuman; the beacon of glory
beckoning all to participate in Shiva's feast.

5

On this night of our *Mahadeva* -
the creator of Brahma, Vishnu, Indra,
the essence It-Self whom all worship -
those who can focus their thoughts on Shiva
can achieve knowledge and powers divine.

The temple dancers performed *tandava nritya*
depicting how the master of flux,
the end and the beginning of all things,
danced his steps of destruction and regeneration;
how Shiva swallowed the poison of our world
and bottled it in his throat for our benefit;
how he held the mighty Ganges on his head
or how Ganesha acquired his elephant's head.

While myths and legends stretched my notions of humanity,
the *Atman* revealed itself to be not this, nor that!

6

It would be a gift to meet you, Shiva,
in the Himalayas with Parvati, Kartika and Ganesha.
That journey I hope to make before my time is up,
but tonight I'll settle for a glimpse of you
in any place you care to visit in London.

With your dread-locked hair,
your tiger-skin mini-skirt
pinned in place by snakes coiled around you,
your third eye shining like aurora borealis.
Drum in one hand, *trishul* in the other,
your rhythmic dance would be quite an ethnic
performance *par excellence* in public
with Parvati break-dancing down Trafalgar Square
looking cool in her garland, chic with human heads!

7

If you do decide to answer my prayer,
stop for a moment only your
centuries of meditation;
I will be waiting here
patiently keeping my solitary
vigil for your coming!
Om Namah Shivayam!

The phone rings
and I hear a strange voice say:
This is Shiva speaking...

Notes:

Lingaraja: Lord of the *lingam*, one of Shiva's many names
lingam: the phallic symbol representing Shiva; *yoni*: the female organ
masala: mixture of spices; *arati*: waving of a lamp, etc. before an image in worship
tulsi: basil, a sacred plant; *bel-patri*: the wood-apple leaf which is sacred to Shiva
diya: lamp; *Mahadeva*: Great god, one of Shiva's names
tandava nritya: Shiva's cosmic dance; *Atman*: Soul; *trishul*: trident

MY GOOD LUCK HOME

You presented me with two scarabs,
hieroglyphs etched on their lapis-lazuli backs,
from the gift-shop of the British Museum.

It's for good luck, you said;
I surveyed the pieces, their sacredness
treasured in the hollow of my palm,
imagining them alive, at home in a desert.

They nestled behind a coral stone and a pearl
framed in rings of beaten gold on my fingers;
charms given by my family to protect me from evil.

I find the Egyptian scarab couple their own home
away from the crowded open-house of my Indian gods,
transforming each corner of my living room
with the gifts of fetishes from around the world.

Two Chinese cats guard my speculative angle of vision.
Even Ganesha travels with me in my handbag
to help me overcome obstacles in my adopted homeland.

The seven gods of luck from Japan smile on
as you eye my marble turtle god with its fine chiselled look,
its beady eyes, hand-crafted, appraising your secret nook -
leaving us with the legacy of an understanding -

The knowledge of what it means
to carry a whole household in oneself,
to be so perfectly self-contained, poised
at the centre of all manner of creatures unsheltered.

SHAFI AHMED

BEDEH

This is the name of my clan.
I am a water-gypsy
on the turbulent rivers of Bangladesh.
My boat is home
to me, my wife, and our children.

I have some knowledge of words
and wild herbs.
I treat snake-bites,
drive out evil spirits,
and attempt things which others dare not.
Tigers, robbers, snakes, demons, storms
all seem to leave me alone!

My needs are small and simple.
They are easily met
from day to day,
from hand to mouth,
from one river-bend settlement
to the next.

Sometimes in fine weather
I row out to the river's end.
I meet many ships at the anchorage.
The crew exchange foodstuffs,
old clothes, newspapers,
empty cans and bottles
with my beads, bangles,
bamboo-toys and sea shells.

Once I had a chance to board
an English ship.
I marvelled at the ocean-going craft.
But the Captain, he marvelled: at me,
at the size of my boat,
at how we had survived, and at how we live!

He wrote down our names,
and other things in his notebook.
He said, one day he would write about us.
I cannot imagine
why would anyone want
to do that!

BULU'S FREEDOM

She was a distant niece.
An only child of her parents.
Her father died when she was one
and her mother at three.
At four she was blinded
because there was no disinfectant
to wash down her eyes.
But she was a pretty, happy child
growing up with other children
in an extended family
in rural Bangladesh.

When she was about ten, I saw her
in one of my flying five-yearly visits
to the ancestral homestead.
She was talking with other children
glowing with excitement of kinship,
"He is my uncle... from London...
rich... has a big car..."
I moved out of earshot
in acute embarrassment.

She did not actually ask me for a thing!
Money, sweets, toys, a pretty frock...
Nothing!
I only discussed these matters
perfunctorily,
with my cousin,
her legal guardian.

On my next visit
I heard she was dead.
Cholera got her.
She did not even have a grave.
Floods had washed down
the whole burial ground by the river
to the sea,
and to God.

SHENAZ ALI

A BROKEN HEART

A broken heart,
and the worst part,
he promised not to break it.

He took and flew,
and the only clue
was he promised not to take it.

Though a million times he lied,
my true feelings never died.

I don't know how to handle pain.
It hurts too much to risk again.

The reason why I cannot sleep:
my hurt inside is much too deep.

We were finished from the start
as he tore my world apart.
Grin and bear it? I can't fake it.

A broken heart,
and the worst part,
he promised not to break it.

He took and flew,
and the only clue
was he promised not to take it.

MONIZA ALVI

TAKEAWAY

Our customer has faith in our foil containers,
our steam - that she takes away as easily

as raindrops on her new coat.
But notice how her life stands still,

neither warming, nor cooling.
She is expecting something to happen

before the grains of rice harden.
She is waiting - For a train?

A baby? A job? For the new world?
She has forgotten what she is waiting for.

We must take her inside
where it is bitter and golden with turmeric,

lead her where our bowls and spoons
scoop up the indoor air,

and the sun enters like an angel,
brightening our sauces.

Let us take her in case she has a pain,
in case the menu is longer than her life.

Let's donate her our burgundy curtains.
Our undefinable smells.

The remnants of our country.

QUEEN-OF-THE-NIGHT

The young woman in her bedroom
with her forest-heavy heart
feels as if she's trying to please
all the countries of the world at once -
Stand under my torrential rains,
listen to the hissing of my branches.

But the young woman invents
her own story, stitching it in the dark.

Parents reminisce about sleeping on the roof,
tell her how the miraculously scented
Queen-of-the-night opens
its starfish flowers in the dark.
But they're happier now in New Malden
where it's cleaner, inviting
professional people to dinner.
They no longer take hot milk with tea.

The young woman views the curtains
billowing, first with duty, then desire,
wishes she could dance lightly
from one land to another, or launch
her life like a ship, out to sea, or further.

Her own territory -
a box of jewels, or fireworks.
A walk in the park. Silver leaves.

THOUGHTS OF A PAKISTANI WOMAN
IN AN ENGLISH JAIL

It's true, I'm happier than before.
Here, for the first time I know I'm me,
not this man's daughter, that man's wife.

My crime? I had no choice.
This wasn't understood.

My own thoughts
swoop like birds around my cell,
almost slipping through the bars.

Thankfully, they are not
Asian birds, or English birds.
At night I count each brilliant feather.

This feather is my will.
That feather is my right.

SHAMIM AZAD

ECLIPSE OF MOONLIGHT

I had a skill
when I jumped ship.
I grabbed
a fistful of earth,
took a deep breath and looked
towards the cold grey valley
in the distance,
on this island.

I am one of those women
who can recognise
an unknown city,
one of the map-makers,
the nomads.

I knew where
the shore was
in the eclipse of moonlight -
the seagulls' nests.

I could smell raw fish,
lime and timber;
the ragged people
and I became one.

I predicted the possibilities
of rainfall, the whirling storm,
and of sprinkling spices
wherever they were needed.
Now, I have lost it all.

TWOFOLD

No, I wasn't blessed with twins.
I often wonder how it feels
to be a mother of twice-the-same -
a pair of feel-alike-children.

I suppose
they have a language of their own,
a self-made dome,
a town full of life-given toys
and a balloon
that flies up and down,
on an invisible string held
in one's hand.

I think
when I had my daughter,
I felt as if
I was a twin of her's
and there she was,
my double.
The cloud of loneliness,
the tremendous urge to become mute,
simply evaporated.

Since her birth
neither of us has cried.
I have felt protected
as if in our own castle.
The lovely auburn hair,
the fringe on her tiny forehead,
empowered my connections
like sparkling waves.
She brought comfort
and independence.

In her teens
those crystal-clear never-resolving
debates we had,
made me her other half.
Without her
I was incomplete.

Now when she is a woman,
the twinship promises so much,
I am almost brimming
with arrogance.

It scares me.
The thought of being
double and then half,
is killing me
because I have to be the first to go -
leaving her behind.

MARIYA AZIZ

SOLITUDE

Withdrawing from the eye of the world,
I crave the sweet bliss of solitude.

ALIEN ABDUCTION

Snatched away on a not quite round silver saucer
To a world unknown, far away and alien -
To me.

Abducted from my world.
What for?
"For your own good, for education, for ...,"
They said.

They called this world England:
Small, contained, powerful
And surrounded by sea.

A solitary world inside a world -
Like me.

One of my kind -
Or so I felt.
Searching eyes and hostile glances
Scoured me each and every day,
Questioning my right to be here.

I was different:
A black-haired, brown-eyed
Blot in a white sea.

It took time for me to understand
That, alien as this country was to me,
An alien is what I was to them.
Would I ever be anything else?

DILEEP BAGNALL

IF YOU JUMP

If you jump
off the cliff
you can fly
or fall

either way
the cliff remains

to climb
fly back to
abandon
or ignore

NEGOTIATIONS

we haggle
split the indifference
and you leave

to appropriate
someone else's sunshine

NOT PARANOID BUT PRACTICAL

To escape the assassins
I find a psychiatrist
and feign schizophrenia.

He is pleased I take
the medication.
And I bide my time.

Pretending I hear things.
Waiting to be sprung
by the SAS.

RAJAT KUMAR BISWAS

CAMBRIDGE

(*In memory of David Rushton*)

Seventh of January, 'fifty-three,
was a white letter day for me
because it was then that I learnt to hitchhike,
a word hitherto unknown in
my dictionary; my pal Cambridge,
cap-a-pie, wrapping himself with
his old college scarf, led me
as the lighted first tube train
disgorged us at daybreak in Hendon.

'That side is Wales and all the world
beyond, this side is England,' my comrade
opined; a shudder went down my spine
as, priest-like in my Pa's nineteen
twenty-nine style topcoat, I stood
with rubber-soled Dolcis
shoes, upon the pristine snow,
in a totally unused, Bengali way.

We hitched, thumbed and thumbed
as, slowly, my toes got numb:
'Biswas, say some Bengali slang!'
At the acme of exasperation,
a new red Austin gave a lift.
Icicles hung on the trees, the wind
swished over the cables, crows flapped
their black wings.

At last the hitching succeeded, this time
a truck-driver reduced speed, stopped.
My friend asked me to squeeze in
between his spread-eagled thighs,
leaving room for the driver's mate.
To break the ice, the driver
asked, 'what work do you
do?' Although a library student,
my pal said, 'I am a librarian';
for my private ear he said,

'otherwise these people would not
understand, I had to say so'.
At a transport cafe (loud
with a juke-box - a novelty)
where the driver parked,
my colleague warned, 'Don't give
to the lift-giver any baksheesh,
it isn't done by the English'.

SEPTEMBER, 1987

These apples which were windfall
have now been picked, our good neighbours
would not mind if we use them.
It is a season when mellowing fruits
welcome the onset of cooler days' imprints
upon the entwined purple Virginia creepers;
the hanging baskets of pink and white starry geraniums,
and healthy, rounded fuchsia bulbs
drive the message, 'tis time to bring the plants inside the room
or the onset of inclement Autumn
weather becomes harmful.
Upon the uncut wet grass, my pair of Hush-Puppies
trod ankle-deep; silently the birds
ate the berries.
Upon the tool shed door the pair of snails lay vertically, snug
under their brown, striped shells.
Over the compost heap a few earth-worms
zigzagged, good omen for the gardener.

The last night of the Proms over,
and at Chelmsford the cricket season ending -
whose win would you prefer?

SINDAMANI BRIDGLAL

SHE LIVES BETWEEN BACK HOME AND HOME

She lives between back home and home
Frantic
Desire mingling with unease as she
Carved a space for you
Kindled a spirit that would guard against
The despair of her life
And the desire for you to be
What she could not be
Frightened she pushed
You away from her
And frightened
Held you too close
Daughters were to give
Mothers
A sense of themselves.

VARUN CHANDRA

BEE

The striped plane leaves the runway
Of a bustling, sticky port,
A gentle roar from the engine
Tickling the eardrums as it overtakes,
Bouncing on the sheets of sunlight.
It scours the area,
Flying low,
Pausing for fuel
Now and again.
As it settles, it picks its spot,
Drawing on invisible blood;
Abruptly hopping on
To rest in the haven
Of colourful fingers.
Approach it -
The angry gunfire resumes,
Hackles raised,
Antennae tensed.
The chase begins:
Flying, running, turning, swirling, drifting

And stinging.

DEBJANI CHATTERJEE

TO THE ENGLISH LANGUAGE

Indifferent language of an alien shore,
the journey was troubled but I am here:
register me among your step-children.

That special love that flows easy with my birth-right
is for Bengali, my mother - a well rounded tongue,
sweet and juicy with monsoon warmth,
rich and spicy with ancestral outpourings.

What has proficiency to do with it?
I know I dream it endlessly.

English, your whiplash of thoughts
has scarred me, pebbles rattle in my mouth
while innuendoes turn my tongue.

For generations you called to me,
siren of the seven western seas,
though now you may deny this and tell me
to go back where I came from.
Your images were the barbed lines
that drew me, torn, to this island keep.

Your words raise spectral songs to haunt me.
I have subverted your vocabulary
and mined rebellious corridors of sound.
I have tilled the frozen soil of your grammar
- I will reap the romance of your promises.

I know you now
with the persistence that a stranger musters.
I know the madness hidden in your rules and relics,
I see the glory where you would disown it.
I know my own desperate yearning,
but I do not come to your rhythms empty-handed
- the treasures of other traditions are mine,
so many koh-i-noors, to be claimed.

It is now my turn to call you at my homecoming.
I have learnt to love you
- the hard way.

Note:
Koh-i-noor: an Indian diamond which graces the British crown.

VISITING E M FORSTER

"But Forster doesn't live here any more."
I knew that of course. He died the year before
- before my passage. I told 'Raised Eyebrows'
that I only wanted ... to see his room,
to see the view. Why else would I have come?
"But this is not a museum, you know."
(Cambridge, not a museum?) I nodded.
"An ordinary room." Ordinary
is what it takes. I remembered my coach
journey from Canterbury. "I have come
all the way from India. He was my friend."
It worked. The brows subsided, defeated.

A bemused stranger occupied the place
- half apologised for everything changed.
The room was functional, anonymous:
he could not have lived here long. "I'm afraid
even the furniture is not the same."
What did I care, standing at the window.
Olive groves beside the forget-me-not
Mediterranean rolled below, with
a dust haze veiling the Marabar curves.
"It is the same," I said, "nothing has changed."

NOT YOUR AVERAGE SNAKE

I'm not your average snake in the grass,
I don't slither shiver any old spine.
   I am the speckled band
    that ornaments the hand,
delicately dispensing decisions
of life and death by Manasa Devi.

I'm not your apple-tempting sneak serpent.
I don't seduce those innocent of shame.
   I am the quick thinking,
    quivering, day-saving,
prayer-knot round Ganesha's pot belly,
holding contentment, jam-packed and spilling.

I'm not the viper battering Heaven,
injecting venom with my fruity words.
   I am the effortless,
    cooling, clinging, necklace,
twined to comfort Shiva's blue martyred throat.
We are twin kings, dancing in ecstasy.

I'm not the fanged beast reigning over Hell,
striking fear with forked and flickering tongue.
   I am the tireless rope;
    my turning is the hope
of gods and demons churning the ocean.
I, Vasuki, raise order from chaos.

Notes:

Manasa Devi: Snake Goddess

Ganesa: Elephant-headed God of Wisdom

Vasuki: giant serpent used by the gods and demons to churn the ocean and gather its
treasures. The venom released by Vasuki was swallowed by the Destroyer God, Shiva,
turning his throat blue. Shiva is also called Neelkantha (the blue-throated) and Nataraja
(King of Dance).

SAMIR CHATTERJEE

HILLSBOROUGH

Saw you at the turnstiles by the park;
Fresh-faced, beaming with smile,
Ready to conquer the world.
You always believed:
There was no Alps before Hannibal's men.

It was to be an afternoon of sporting excellence.
Stars would polish the sky that night.
You were to write letters of celebration
In colours of fire.
Your hopes and joys were infectious.

You gathered behind the goal mouth,
Penned behind barriers with other hopefuls,
In your desire to welcome your heroes
As they break through the ultimate defence
Of the vanquished.

Sombrely the park shook.
An almighty roar split the stadium,
Sparking an avalanche of bodies.
Strange limbs squeezed every inch of you.
You fought to shake off their dead weight.
When the earth vanished from under your feet,
You looked for your mum from the heat of the cage.

Sought for help in despair;
There was no ambulance in sight.
Beside you there were others
Sickened below the entangled limbs,
Desperate for a glimpse of blue sky.
Their disappearing hands
Waving farewell to the universe.

The caretakers of the ground were silent.
They blamed you for killing yourself.
Laying you and your friends in the morgue,
They flashed their cameras repeatedly
To make a quick kill in the media next day.

The sweat on your face was still warm.
Devoid of the crushing pain,
It glowed in tender innocence,
Posing a fiery question to the park keepers:
'Did you have to snatch my life so soon?'

They are still struggling for an answer -
Years later.
Millions have echoed your call.
Your voice from the valley of death
Rises to a crescendo. It will not stop
Until the secret doors of the system
Are torn down and the culprits apprehended.

I never thought you would walk alone.

MARY DAMMYENTY CHAUHAN

MY MOTHER

My mother,
      roundness
            of face.

The moon shines,
raw circles of umber.
Tortoise-shell cat.
Two semi-circles glued together.
A gold signet ring on
a plump mid finger,
never
    did
        get it engraved.

It proudly took the place
of a wedding ring.

Hot,
    brown
        baked skin.

Bursting, spitting... roasting.
On cold days... she
looked sunflower yellow,
margarine, camel... sad.

Naru (rope) mark around her waist,
pink flesh clashes with the brown.
Sometimes bleeding, sometimes sore,
never did see her
        cry then.
Nails full of snuff.
Sari like the sea.
Sergeant major growl, stout and strict.
Authoritarian with warmest affection.
Never got round to a set of dentures.
Protective, defenceless as a child.
Back to square one,
senile dementia.

Pickle jars, spiced mangoes in dark cupboards.
Rolling poppadoms and drying them
on the outside table,
until they baked hard in the sun.

BETEL NUT

Mother chewed the paan,
  chanut ni patra,
until her tongue was burning bright,
a curious shade of henna.

Chalk and *supari* were bad for the teeth.
Tobacco in small portions was used in
respectable form, along with the
sweetened *waliari*.

She, she... introduced me
to the ritual of folding,
massaging the *chuno* until it
outlined thin cabbage veins
of the stem.

I, I... observed swimming movements
of the hand,
gliding like a fish,
smothered in bewilderment.

I listened to her crack the cardamom
pods, stuck in her tooth,
looking like freckles of rye
and, carry on talking to my father,
a human in skeleton form,
capable of living without lime.

Notes:

chanut ni patra: *paan* or betel leaf
supari: betel or areca nut
waliari: fennel
chuno: lime

MAYA CHOWDHRY

BRIDES OF DUST

There are rooms in Pakistan which avoid me, old stone houses
carved from exile. At night the stone transforms
and women's voices cry, their smooth skin blends
into sandstone tomb.

She wears red chillies in her hair,
walks 30 miles for water and returns
to find her children turned to dust.
The rain is a gift she has not received,
death finds places to talk to her, her mother's songs
are her grandmother's dreams, her daughter's nightmares.

There are flames and silence in these houses,
the sandstone women are married
to death. An old woman painted my hands
like a virgin bride while I searched in her eyes for a flicker of belonging.

Three nights and two cultures I wandered in desert
lands, dreaming of sandstone women in village
houses, digging for roots, ginger and
religion. Her head is sprinkled with water,
cleansing she passes prasad to her daughter,
two hands, blessing. In the mirrors
of her kameez she watches
the eyes of sandstone women narrow and close.

She remembers her mother never
cut her hair, she remembers
it coarse and grey, she remembers the eyes
of sandstone women, she remembers three cultures,
two nights, that roots make a difference. In her first language
she learns to say mother, in her second home, she remembers
sandstone women, in her dreams she goes home with them.

The boundaries of land shatter memory,
there is no map to lead my family
home. They travel to voices
and words become death. The colour of my roots

makes me shout. I am located in earth,
my feet have no voice, I am located in sound, I walk into language.

There are marriage rooms
in this story. She has more language
than difference, she speaks root words,
looks for rivers in the desert,
knows places to die with sandstone women, closes her eyes.

MY EYES

I'm looking at the tower blocks of Hulme, holding up the sky,
and every 15 seconds the picture changes, smog catches
the back of my throat, coughing I look out at a Delhi skyline,
ragged and dusty, I have to shut my left eye to return to England.

My right eye composes Internet adverts that travel the Web, goes
dancing at the Hacienda, wears 10 denier, loves men.
My left eye drives a rickshaw, eats paan at 5am, loves women.
My right eye comes home to tortillini with spinach and ricotta, puts
on a CD of Portishead and crashes out in a crescendo of 70's revival.
My left eye objects, buys pani puri on the corner of Janpath Market,
while 'Chaltie, Chaltie' from Pakeezah blares out from a trashed
radio wedged between the boiling oil and a pan of chai.

I shut both eyes, wanting release, tired of reliving the collision
at Defence Colony between an auto-rickshaw driver
and a tourist's taxi going South.

Note:
Pakeezah: A popular Hindi movie. 'Chaltie, Chaltie' is one of its songs.

WHAT IS RACISM?

A Black man, on the bus one seat ahead,
scalp shaved to the skin
has a 4 inch scar etched from
his left to his right ear.
Do you think -
a) He was stabbed in a gangland fight.
b) He's had a tumour removed from his brain.
c) His mother dropped him at 6 months.

An Asian taxi driver picks you up
from the station, you're tired and he can't understand
where you're heading.
Do you think -
a) It's nice to see immigrant working for a change.
b) He's stolen future generation's work.
c) Get off on the corner of Brightside and Scott Road,
and walk the rest of the way home.

An African woman stands on a street corner
in a white lacy, crotch high dress.
Do you think -
a) She's been stood up by her white boyfriend.
b) She's a pro ... I mean sex-worker.
c) How nice the dress looks on her.

What is Racism ?
The answer is a, b or c ?

SALEHA CHOWDHURY

A BOTTLE OF PERFUME

She's got a bottle of
Perfume.
It's the memory of her first love.
That lovely, catchy, melodious tune.
She married the man.
A big house,
No family plan.
A big dining table
Sits about a dozen.

From the bottom drawer
Of a chest
She gets her bottle out.
In her dented mood
And depressive bout,

Sprays the perfume all over
To renew the torn licence
Of marriage
Once more, forever.

EXISTENTIALISM

A mountain
Had a go at a
Tiny speck of dust.
'What is my fault?'
The tiny speck asked.
'Listen,' the mountain roared,
'You are not a part of me,
Still a free soul
Among the grass.'

DAVID DABYDEEN

COOLIE ODYSSEY
for Ma, d. 1985

Now that peasantry is in vogue,
Poetry bubbles from peat bogs,
People strain for the old folk's fatal gobs
Coughed up in grates North or North East
'Tween bouts o' living dialect,
It should be time to hymn your own wreck,
Your house the source of ancient song:
Dry coconut shells cackling in the fireside
Smoking up our children's eyes and lungs,
Plantains spitting oil from a clay pot,
Thick sugary black tea gulped down.

The calves hustle to suck,
Bawling on their rope but are beaten back
Until the cow is milked.
Frantic children call to be fed.
Roopram the Idiot goes to graze his father's goats backdam
Dreaming that the twig he chews so viciously in his mouth
Is not a twig.

In a winter of England's scorn
We huddle together memories, hoard them from
The opulence of our masters.

You were always back home, forever
As canefield and whiplash, unchanging
As the tombstones in the old Dutch plot
Which the boys used for wickets playing ball.

Over here Harilall who regularly dodged his duties at the marketstall
To spin bowl for us in the style of Ramadhin
And afterwards took his beatings from you heroically
In the style of England losing
Is now known as the local Paki
Doing slow trade in his Balham cornershop.
Is it because his heart is not in business
But in the tumble of wickets long ago
To the roar of wayward boys?

Or is it because he spends too much time
Being chirpy with his customers, greeting
The tight-wrapped pensioners stalking the snow
With tropical smile, jolly small chat, credit?
They like Harilall, these muted claws of Empire,
They feel privileged by his grinning service,
They hear steelband in his voice
And the freeness of the sea.
The sun beams from his teeth.

Heaped up beside you Old Dabydeen
Who on Albion Estate clean dawn
Washed obsessively by the canal bank,
Spread flowers on the snake-infested water,
Fed the gods the food that Chandra cooked,
Bathed his tongue of the creole
Babbled by low-caste infected coolies.
His Hindi chants terrorised the watertoads
Flopping to the protection of bush.
He called upon Lord Krishna to preserve
The virginity of his daughters
From the Negroes,
Prayed that the white man would honour
The end-of-season bonus to Poonai
The canecutter, his strong, only son:
Chandra's womb being cursed by deities
Like the blasted land
Unconquerable jungle or weed
That dragged the might of years from a man.
Chandra like a deaf-mute moved about the house
To his command,
A fearful bride barely come-of-age
Year upon year swelling with female child.
Guilt clenched her mouth
Smothered the cry of bursting apart:
Wrapped hurriedly in a bundle of midwife's cloth
The burden was removed to her mother's safekeeping.
He stamped and cursed and beat until he turned old
With the labour of chopping tree, minding cow, building fence
And the expense of his daughters' dowries.
Dreaming of India
He drank rum

Till he dropped dead
And was buried to the singing of Scottish Presbyterian hymns
And a hell-fire sermon from a pop-eyed bawling catechist,
By Poonai, lately baptised, like half the village.

Ever so old,
Dabydeen's wife,
Hobbling her way to fowl-pen,
Cussing low, chewing her cud, and lapsed in dream,
Sprinkling rice from her shrivelled hand.
Ever so old and bountiful,
Past where Dabydeen lazed in his mudgrave,
Idle as usual in the sun,
Who would dip his hand in a bowl of dhall and rice -
Nasty man, squelching and swallowing like a low-caste sow -
The bitch dead now!

The first boat chugged to the muddy port
Of King George's Town. Coolies come to rest
In El Dorado,
Their faces and best saris black with soot.
The men smelt of saltwater mixed with rum.
The odyssey was plank between river and land,
Mere yards but months of plotting
In the packed bowel of a white man's boat
The years of promise, years of expanse.

At first the gleam of the green land and the white folk and the Negroes,
The earth streaked with colour like a toucan's beak,
Kiskidees flame across a fortunate sky,
Canefields ripening in the sun
Wait to be gathered in armfuls of gold.

I have come back late and missed the funeral.
You will understand the connections were difficult.
Three airplanes boarded and many changes
Of machines and landscapes like reincarnations
To bring me to this library of graves,
This small clearing of scrubland.
There are no headstones, epitaphs, dates.
The ancestors curl and dry to scrolls of parchment.
They lie like texts

Waiting to be written by the children
For whom they hacked and ploughed and saved
To send to faraway schools.
Is foolishness fill your head.
Me dead.
Dog-bone and dry-well
Got no story to tell.
Just how me born stupid is so me gone.
Still we persist before the grave
Seeking fables.
We plunder for the maps of El Dorado
To make bountiful our minds in an England
Starved of gold.

Albion village sleeps, hacked
Out between bush and spiteful lip of river.
Folk that know bone
Fatten themselves on dreams
For the survival of days.
Mosquitoes sing at a nipple of blood.
A green-eyed moon watches
The rheumatic agony of houses crutched up on stilts
Pecked about by huge beaks of wind,
That bear the scars of ancient storms.
Crappeau clear their throats in hideous serenade,
Candleflies burst into suicidal flame.
In a green night with promise of rain
You die.

We mark your memory in songs
Fleshed in the emptiness of folk,
Poems that scrape bowl and bone
In English basements far from home,
Or confess the lust of beasts
In rare conceits
To congregations of the educated
Sipping wine, attentive between courses -
See the applause fluttering from their fair hands
Like so many messy table napkins.

KETAKI KUSHARI DYSON

TO JENNY JOSEPH

'When I am an old woman I shall wear purple ...'

— Jenny Joseph, 'Warning'

But Jenny, I already wear purple,
swathes of purple, cascades of pimiento-red,
and all the bold patterns that looms and needles unfold,
so what shall I do when I am old?

I swear to you, I have a sari of luminous silk
where purple sea-waves beat upon beaches of gold,
and one which is a jade river, in whose estuary
ride the ten incarnations of Vishnu - a majestic bestiary.

I carry all that on myself, and let others do the staring.
I sit down on floors, on pavements, on thresholds of houses.
I surprise stiff air hostesses by asking for whisky and ice.
Waiting for my suitcase, I sit on the bottom of my trolley.

When the sun beats down, I carry a parasol,
which no one does in Kidlington, and when I hear thunder
and the trip switch going 'tock', turning off my computer,
I rush out in sandals, in slippers - to welcome the rain.

I buy the most chequered, the largest extra-bright shirts,
and hats with pink roses from seedy second-hand shops,
and when the north wind blows my roses away
I run after them and rescue them from the road.

I tell you, Jenny, what I shall *not* do when I am old.
I shall never eat three pounds of sausages at a go.
But I shall chop onion, chillies, and coriander
and pile it all on dollops of peanut butter on toast.

I already hoard earrings and things in inlaid boxes,
I have taught my children to be polite and not to swear,
stood cooking for my friends till all my arches have fallen
and the sheep come home in despair.

Once I fell flat on the steps of a gallery in Bonn
and was told off for wanting to bring in a bag

with paper, and pen, and mints to suck against thirst -
it was against the rules, and that was that.

When I am an old woman, I shall sail to Iceland in a boat
and speak to eagles, if there be any left.
From a snug cottage window I shall watch Hekla spit fire
and chalk my last poem on a square of wood-framed slate.

HERB-THOUGHTS

Born amongst people who free themselves by fire,
I had a horror of burial - its box,
rotting in it, being licked by worms.
Ashes seemed such a cleaner terminal.

At the same time, by a poet's paradox,
I loved grave-tops in quiet country places,
happy to bless their leaning, coded stones,
or stroke, in green humps, their spent ecstasies.

A year's staring at a raised bed of herbs,
which my son helped to build, shaped like an outsize grave,
makes me reflect that nature's scorification
under such growth is no abominable fate.

My chives are fat. My thyme is spruce and spiky.
The mint, a violinist's gift, suffers no rust.
The lemon balms are well in tune. The sage
is as healthy as a voice singing *Toreador* ...

Sweet marjoram, discarded by another,
bold and golden, is wholly at home.
Autumn's squat refugee, graciously resettled,
knows, by spring's mirror, how tall she's grown.

The dry rosemary remembers and waits.
So do I, and carefully have sown
the year's coriander, ready for the rain.
Hopefully the tiny wombs will open.

The parsley has packed, though when stiffly camped
late last summer, it had looked fighting enough.

This twisted bush, my mother-in-law had cracked,
will do its best in the shade of a nagging wife.

But since you died, Mum,
in hard February, when frost was on the ground,
I gave up nagging your son, mothered him instead.
So the poor parsley grieved and grew into its grave.

Beyond all belief, my sleek, sour-leafed sorrels
have become the green light of the yard.
If I die, lay me by a hawthorn
and scatter a packet of sorrel seeds on the earth.

Spring sorrel, wild as my sorrow, and already seeding,
self-digesting: let your juices work in me.
Endorse me, so I can't go wrong. Ink
to ink. Leaves to leaves. Mourning to mourning.

Cleave me with your roots
till all my fibres are displaced
and only my bones are left
in your dark embrace.

GENDER, ETHNICITY, COMMUNITY

José speaks to me in the street,
so does Kwan, when I spy him.
They don't try to avoid my eyes,
but wave to me cheerily
from the street's other side.

José is handsome:
he used to run the local fish and chips.
He owns it still, but has someone else managing it,
and has bought himself another shop in a nearby village,
where he now spends more time,
managing the big fish and the little fish.

His mother came from Buenos Aires,
and his kids are fluent in the local English
while holding on to their Spanish papers,
pasaportes, as he calls them - with pride.

José asks me about my activities
in detail, with courtesy. He is proud to chat
with someone who writes books, and wins prizes,
travels, and has been to Buenos Aires,
whose play is performed
in this country and abroad.

He advises me I must have real holidays too,
not just travel in connection with my work -
don't I think I need a break? -
and what about that fellow who stole from my book -
did the law bring him to heel, or what?

Ah, law, that magniloquent futility,
that masquerade, that fraud,
where principles don't matter
and all the games are bought.
Well, you have to get the dosh how you can,
briefing, de-briefing, thieving -
so long as you don't get caught -

juggling, sword-swallowing, writing,
fiddling, fire-eating, fishing,
at least running a fish and chips shop,
while high, high on an overarching bridge,
lean, laughing, and taut,
sits the angel who is angling for us all:
Death, the supreme *pescador*.

Kwan is good-looking too, and older,
and well-informed;
he knows all about Borneo
and business and politics and economics.
He had world-wide connections
long before the Internet
and is always asking me to make a halt
in his native, torrid, arboreous part of the world,
make a holiday of it, why not.

He used to own a store right in our street once -
it was my lifeline for groceries -
but it was more and more work

for less and less cash,
so he sold it while he could
to retire early and live in ease
with his wife, who is English,
and his daughters, who belong only in this country
and nowhere else.

Now, master of his own time,
buoyant, neither with nor against the tide,
he surveys the follies of this
narrowed nineties world
with unerring Chinese eyes.

I am making a quick mental scan
of other men who speak to me in the street ...
With most men you know what it's like -
like double yellow lines -
no talking in the street.

There are the women, of course.
After twenty-eight years in the same place
there's got to be a few women
who speak to you in the street.

There are four or five Englishwomen,
each with her predominant passion,
the tense woman from Belfast,
the jolly Welshwoman from Swansea,
the black woman round the corner
who's always in her dressing-gown, moaning,
the inquisitive Jewess from Karachi ...

Some of the husbands will nod, when face to face.
The violin teacher will speak
if you catch him on his front lawn -
he always asks about our younger son, whom he taught.
The Jewess' husband is a Caribbean -
he used to talk aplenty in the past;
but now he's an old lion, doesn't see well,
passes you quietly by, clutching a shopping-bag.
The Irishman taught me to drive -
he's always encased in his car

earning his living,
so you may glimpse him passing
but he's never free
to talk to you in the street.

Ah yes, there was Tom,
Tom the poet, the angler,
who hailed from the Lake District.
I knew him well, and his wife. Once upon a time
we showed each other our poems
and went to workshops together
in his red Swedish car.
He taught me about a whole new genre
of poetry - fishing-poems -
and he always talked to me in the street

except when he was depressed,
when he was no company,
like an owl disturbed in its sleep,
but now he is gone, gone,
fished by the supreme fisherman,

and I've been to the funeral
in the local Anglican temple -
in a black Poona sari
with green and purple dots -
Tom, you didn't see me -
how elegant I looked - you would have approved -
so really

José and Kwan,
Kwan and José
are now the only men left who have time
to speak to me in the street.

JEANNE ELLIN

A GIFT FOR GRANDMOTHER

Since I cannot know

Since I cannot know how you came together
Nor what it was you felt towards that man
Of another race and tongue, his mind formed
And fed on conqueror's meat, I can only

Speculate, count the possibilities like
Prune stones round a plate. Coercion,
Commerce, compliance, need, greed or
Perhaps just a price agreed. Yet still

I will hope your bodies bridged with
Gentle touch and stranger's smiles, I
will hope your minds reached beyond
Alien skin and found a wordless core

Of trust, even though its grace lasted
Only until your bodies peeled apart.

GRANDMOTHER

You brought a heritage of songs and dreams, but they were
Left to decay within your open palms, as your children turned
Their faces from your dark gaze, and stopped their ears to your
Stories, longing only for their father's powerful pallor.

They let your name decay unused, smothered you with silence,
Ignored your presence and denied the very rumour of your
Life. So impoverished, I cannot search out your home, learn
Your stories nor hear your songs, or honour your faith.

Leaving me the only gift of yours that denial could not
Quench. These rich tints of hair and skin that link me
Irrevocably to you. Mark me yours beyond dispute, Dark
Mother I walk in your skin. Your granddaughter at last.

YASMIN FAROOQ

IS BIOLOGY MY DESTINY?

Oh yes, this is my man,
 who dreams I be a 'traditional' woman
 who would almost 'worship' her man,
 would stay at home to look after his offspring,
 bake chapatis, curries, chips and puddings,
 clean the house from top to bottom
 and never complain of boredom.
Oh yes, this is my man.
 After having done everything,
 he would expect me to be smiling
 when he came back from working.
 After all I would only have been
 doing 'housework' and looking after children,
 changing their nappies, bathing them alone.
Oh yes, this is my man.
 Unfortunately, I too am 'officially' working
 to maintain our standard of living.
 He reckons it is leisure for which I'm working.
 It's not surprising and he's not alone in thinking thus,
 though deep down he would not deny
 my financial contribution.
Oh yes, this is my man,
 but confession would put him in an awkward position
 as the 'breadwinner' notion must stay,
 otherwise the whole 'culture' will fade away.
 My earnings must not be spent on food
 or towards the mortgage instalment
 as these are the major components.
Oh yes, this is my man.
 My contribution would therefore mean
 the failure of his duty as a man.
 I am acting as best I can,
 professionally in my own capacity,
 at work and in my ultimate destiny
 as a housewife with agony.
Oh yes, this is my man.
 Both things do have something in common:
 my boss, a white man, also gives me the impression
 that being an Asian woman I am not supposed to have an opinion.

In him racism and sexism combine
and lead to further oppression.
Oh yes, this is my man.
I have to prove to them that I can survive
despite the stress and demands of two separate lives,
where one expects me to be 'flexible',
the other incontrovertible.
But he always finds role models for me,
So-and-so is always better than me.
Oh yes, this is my man.
Once again it is this 'stupid' housework
that divides rather than unites womenfolk.
When questioned about gender inequality,
he would argue that it is biologically
and moreover quite naturally
accepted socially and universally.
Oh yes, this is my man.
He finds my tasks quite satisfactory:
the job, the housework and child care responsibility.
One thing he would not understand quite deliberately:
why I would not smile at him so generously
when he comes home
after a day's 'hard' work.
Oh yes, this is my man.
At work where he is looked after
by one of my purposely appointed sisters
who makes him tea when desired,
dials the telephone when required,
makes appointments as expected.
One thing is clear as far as she is concerned,
Biology is not a destiny for her.
Would he survive without us two?
I tell you the answer is 'no'.
Oh yes, this is my man.

SAQI FAROOQI

THE LIE

Words
      beheading
            words.

But in that hush -
That furious gush of silence
Her maiden speech
Drowned.
She went with it.

During the postmortem
When the knives were out
Carving - n - flensing
The stillborn
Deliberations
The lie was found
Buried in fact
Near cul-de-sac-subconscious
Right across the electric field
Of her magnetic self.

Alive
      indispensable
           intact.

HEART-TRANSPLANT

That:
Willbreaker
Sentimentlauncher
Hatemonger
Lovespinner
Sorrowpumper

That -
Abandoned your bloodport
And landcrashed on
My body terminus
Fresh like a daisy
Fits like a glove
Thank you.

ROMESH GUNESEKERA

FRONTLINERS

(for Shanthi)

House sparrows that shook our pink
blossom loose became enemy
aeroplanes in flight — targets
to the pellet-guns of my childhood.
The war of another age
raged in the mid-afternoon lull
of our shaded veranda
as I culled an imperial culture
from a pile of tatty war-comics
and second-hand adventure stories.
In a post-colonial garden
I grew up
dreaming in English,
biting my tongue.
I made out a Sherwood Forest
of tropicalized longbows,
tommy-gun justice
and an ace James Bond. In those foreign
anachronistic battles
I sided with the language I knew best,
already marked
with a rolling stone's droll beliefs
and in love
with rock an' roll.

Now at the frontline for my new-born
I find myself fighting again —
this time in a language under stress.

TURNING POINT

My host is a monk
from my grandfather's town,

exploring England
in a darkened age.

Stopped temporarily
in a shared room

we meet on my less
noble travels:

discover we are
exactly the same age.

At ten I knew
the world must change;

he, at ten,
also knew the same.

Twenty yards
of saffron robes

captured his boy's
imagination,

while mine slipped
on the slopes

of Tagaytay. He grew
decisive,

unencumbered
in a shaved head;

I became
progressively

less certain,
more curled.

Reaching our mid-thirties
— the age of enlightenment —

he speaks, I listen
only half understanding

this language from my past.
I have stumbled

off the path, tripped
by his inflections.

Once we had
in our Colombo house

a daylight alms-giving
feeding twenty monks.

We served, they ate.
This bright morning

at our breakfast
my laughing monk

serves me
his home-cooking,

turning the tables
in a Manchester flat.

WANDERLUST

Each London high street
has shrunk the earth:
today a spirit of adventure
— call it the migratory instinct
or plain cosmopolitan economics —
spices the fiction
of our floating dreams,
our faint blue fragile
memories of wings.

PRABHU SIDDHARTHA GUPTARA

GLOBAL WARMING

"The moon is gold tonight,
A pleasing colour never seen before.

The moon is gold tonight,
Romantic more than silver ever was.

The moon is gold tonight, my love,
A little less than tinted by the sun."

"Whatever does that mean?" she asked.

"You still have time."

"Still have time?!"

"Yes," he said, "till the neighing of the horse."

"And whatever will I do?" she shrieked,
"The moon turns red."

"There is a rider on the horse," he said:
"The sun!"

ZORINA ISHMAIL-BIBBY

'IMMIGRANT' WOMEN

I like these women's secret faces
Opening and shutting with uncertainty,
Their shy laughter hurled
From overclothed forms,
Muffling out winter,
Rigid as Guys in November
Awaiting the inevitable burn -
Scorch of misunderstanding
Swastika's mark.

They flutter along pavements,
Sparrows hoping to peck
Crumbs of contact.
They are deserted children
Forged unready into marriage,
Mothering, wiving, widowed too soon.
Now, only their sarees' swish
And float over winter boots
Recall their exile from kinder climes.

PASSPORT

Me passport hard and black
As I pass through customs.
I say, yes please, thank you.
Sound right, polite -
British, man, colonised,
I even fool meself
I live here so long,
Fit in, got the externals.
Yet inside, I twist and turn,
Sleep bad, dream plenty.
Tear out me guts, man,
And there I really am.
Wind whistles through me,
Mangrove roots high up
North, here in Britain,
But the rest bury deep
Down by Equator
In Corentyne River.

ADOLESCENCE: GIRL AT JALOUSIE

Warm water Waterloo Street
Jalousies eyed a young girl
Frangipanied in house, stilted
To defend against rains.

Armoured in school uniform,
She tilted at Latin verbs,
Teased out conceits,
Meditated on Hopkins:
"Mind has mountains; cliffs of fall
Frightful, sheer, no-man-fathomed",
Worried bones of alien poems,
Smote scent of her inscape,
Quelled sense of land's glory,
Bird of paradise courting:
Eden at the turn
Before the Fall.

MAHMOOD JAMAL

MIGRANTS

We migrated before we moved,
the gestures that we knew
were sown into new garments;
new words emerged
from our lips.
We learnt to drink
tea from cups
and water in glasses.
Knives and forks
replaced our fingers,
but the cuisine was stubborn
demanding its own etiquette.
Our shoes were laced,
neatly tied up
we were delivered
into the service of a new age
despairing of our inheritance.

We read comics, chewed gum
drank coke from bottles,
watched John Wayne shoot Indians
as we clapped.
Then Marilyn Monroe smiled.
Aftershave arrived
Hollywood style.
The radio blasted us with rock and roll
and we learned to dance
for a dollar or a dime
and signed our future on dotted lines.

We migrated before we moved;
the other place came to us.

ENTRY CERTIFICATE

I enter the big white mansion
a reluctant guest
expected to take his place
like the deferential servant at the gate,
nurtured and well trained
in the art of intimidation and hate.

My stare falls on the trophies
in the hall, photographs, icons, gifts
familiar to me but out of reach.

There is something forbidding in the air.
Though polite and smiling, the inhabitants
transfix me with a stare suggesting
that I should really be elsewhere.

As if these subtle hints
were not enough
they whisper that things might turn rough
not to me of course but they know I'm listening.
The entry sign is lifeless
but the exit blinks and barks.
I too have learnt the art of smiling
enough to make them complacent
as I wait for them
to turn their backs.

SHAHIDAH JANJUA

STRONG AND ANCIENT

I am Diplodocus
Tall and mighty
Strong and ancient.
I am Diplodocus
And I am woman.
You badmouth me
Saying lumbering, saying slut
Saying slow of speed and wit.
What's your hurry?
200 million years I was here
You've only been here two
And in your greed for
All the knowledge
And all the answers
You have sacrificed the world
And your humanity.
You call me animal,
You call me prehistoric.
But I died graceful, peaceful, with dignity
Within the cycle of the seasons,
Within a changing world,
Shrinking seas and rising mountains,
The majesty of which
Dwarf your path to suicide.
I lived 200 million years,
You will but live a few.

MOHAMMAD HAFEEZ JOHAR

HOME

Memories of my homeland. These are burnt into my heart.
But now this city is also in my blood.

So thoughts of the past conjure sadness
through which the present calls to me.

PARM KAUR

THE BREAKING

A black man's sitting
on my uncle's sofa,
never seen one
close up before.

Breaking bones,
they're talking
about breaking bones.

Hockey sticks
into the boot,
folded notes
into his hand.

My cousin's been
'Found out',
tied up,
doors locked.

They're shipping her off
to India, the wedding's
been arranged.

I'm twelve,
not allowed to walk
alone, anymore.

Breaking bones,
they talked
about breaking bones.

DISPLACEMENT

The keepers gather together the stones,
before they themselves turn into dust.

The children of the travellers return
after years of walking on splinters
spewed by those who dispossessed
themselves of their lands.

Splinters of swords their stories
became, as the travellers sought
to forget, struggling to fit
another people's shoes.

The children return to seek
the keepers of the stones,
the grandfathers who hold their stories,
the stones whose heat can release,
can heal their feet.

It is time for the keepers to gather,
to dig up the stones,
pass them on to the children
who return, to piece together
the stories of the land,
of who they were,
who they are.

SHAMSHAD KHAN

OPPRESSED COVERAGE

It's not often you give us prime time slot

but make an exception in time of trouble
when you star us in the news
on ITV *and* BBC

bomb blast it was us who did it
famine the result of Islamic rule
demonstrations only of mindless masses
women covered it's got to be oppressive

and it won't be the last time there's confusion
about Muslims and Islam in this nation
whether on radio or TV
rampaging fundo-oppressive repressives
you know
even I'm starting to get
a negative picture of me

bomb blasts it was us who did it
famine the result of Islamic rule
demonstrations only of mindless masses
women covered it's got to be oppressive

and whatever the news
you restate your views with such ease
always finishing with a call to prayer
Allah-U-Akbar

any excuse to show us on our knees.

SITARA KHAN

THE FOOL'S OBSERVATION

The King at repose, the Queen at her outing,
The Princess in love, the Vizier in anguish,
The Future of the State rests in balance,
Power and treachery contrive a misfortune.
The unsuspecting King could fall for either.
The birds cry pleas of mercy, the rusty red stone
Shudders in fear, tears of blood choke the fountain.
I, a mere Fool, comfort the master.
The humming of voices, the strumming of strings
Heard from afar; sumptuous feasts perfume the air.
True to tradition, the mushaira's prepared.

Note:
mushaira: a gathering of poets

THE KNIGHT

I am resolute
on my stallion.
Velour-skinned, taut-muscled;
In purple, silken paisley *uchhkin*
and *shimla* of organza folds
adorned with amethysts and pearls
and leather *khusa* stitched in gold,
I ride unseen in the thick of the night.

I turn my back on you,
the albatross of duty and honour.
I gallop into the lap of triumph;
I will rescue my Laila
with a trick of my staff.

'Hi! Who goes there?'
'A knight,' say I.
'The night is deep in sleep.'

But Laila lies awake.
I must hurry.
Come, my staff,
Put the guard to sleep.

Notes:
uchhkin: a waistcoat coming down to the thighs
shimla: an elaborate turban with a tufted crest
khusa: hand-stitched leather shoes that are generally richly embroidered
Laila: heroine of the famous story of star-crossed lovers, Laila and Majnoon. Also means 'night' in Arabic.

MOTHER-DAUGHTER

Enveloped in thick blanket of dark hair
Scalp stinging, tears rolling,
Clamped by her feet,
Between my mother's legs I sit.

Tugging, pulling, her dainty hands oiled, combed and disentangled
Their way through the unruly mass.

Ritualistic taming symbolised the plaits.

Weighed by tradition I struggled to be free,
Of bob cut and hair dressers' salons I dared to dream.

School mates' envy brought little relief.
My mother's instinct whispered in my ear:
'Mother's loving milk has nurtured your hair.
In its lustrous length is woven the yarn
From ancestral antiquity to who you now are.
With this dowry I do thee trust
Which for other cares you must not neglect.'

The bonding tie between mother and daughter was such
That scissors of rebellion could never touch.

USHA KISHORE

TEACHING TAGORE TO 10A/S

"Who wanders high on the palace-tower, hair unravelled, unravelled
   Pulling her cloud-blue sari
   Close to her breast?
Who gambols in the shock and flame of the lightning, O who is it
High on the tower today with hair unravelled?"
   - from Rabindranath Tagore's New Rain, translated by William Radice
   and published by Penguin in *Tagore's Selected Poems.*

Tagore drizzles mistily on 10A/S, as my
dusky voice trembles in the monsoon winds;
it is tossed across the stillness of the room,
stifling the questioning looks; it strikes the walls
and its duskier echoes rumble in the corners;
flickering curiosity sparks and lights, gathering
interest soaks the air and scattered smiles seep
into the room...

Floating an Indian poet in an English class,
complemented by sitar music - to be tuned
into ears overflowing with *Anglic* notes and
Saxon beats, seemed ridiculous at first; but
with drumming heart I read, with dancing
eyes, they listen...

I, a relic of the Raj, representing the minority
race, clasp Tagore to my breast and attempt
'Multiculturalism' - a gigantism, knocking
the doors of sleepy classrooms, stumbling
along the corridors of waking schools, perching
precariously on the narrow shelves of dreamy
stockrooms...

Kadamba trees blossom, *ketaki* trees gather
moss and *bakul* trees branch out into the
wilderness, as I wander among the desks,
high on rhythm, low in tone; flashes of doubt
charge the air as these strange words and their
stranger sounds rain in torrents; but then,
'multiculturalism', with a wry smile, thunders

down...

Sitting cross-legged on the table, I watch their
eyes move softly across the page and mumble
zestful words, while my thoughts drift back to
that river bank where I left my water-pot and
my heart...

I show them Tagore as a relief from Donne
and they find a brave new world of dreams
and songs, a hand shoots up: *"Asian women
and hair unravelled? Reformation or Rebellion?"*
I remove my glasses from my eyes - the woman
in the poem is gone - I take her place: *New Rain*
floods my being and rain-clouds wet my eyes, as
Nazeem unveils the purdah of Indian womanhood...

YOU AND ME

You woo my votes and visit my temples and mosques;
you wear my red *tilak* on your forehead and my flower
garlands around your neck; you knock at my door to ask
for more votes and do a disappearing act when I speak of
Kashmir; you say that you believe in the brotherhood of
man and graffiti your white walls with charcoal: *Paki,
go home* - not knowing that *Pak* means pure...

You moan at unpronounceable foreign names and preach
multiculturalism; I teach Steve Biko and Maya Angelou
to your children, who write notes of apology to me:
"Sorry for showing racism to you, Miss..."

You admire my Benares silk saris and my ethnic silver
jewellery and smile at my love for your poetry; I write
my dissertations on Equal Opportunities and you nod
your approval...

At lunch times and breaks, we discuss Jabberwocky
and Godot; my Indian thoughts fire your British hearts and
something in your Englishness warms my Malayalee soul...

And in the mornings, I cut across the *A2* and think of 'You
and Me', beating in time to Kula Shaker's jazzy *"Radha
Ramana Hare, Hare..."*

Notes:
tilak: mark made by anointing the forehead with saffron powder
Malayalee: speaker of Malayalam, the main language spoken in Kerala in India

KHAN SINGH KUMAR

KABBA BARES HIS CHEST AT HIS SON'S PARENTS' EVENING

"What is all this haiku, aiku commotion?
This putting of the comma in the best place?
This Monarchy, shomaky? Dis prayer-business?
Dis telling us that Allah is God? He hasn't
been to his homeland jet so vy tell him da way to Mecca?
Are you making fun of him? Do ju not know
of di assassination of our Gurus?
Now some people debate I'm pundimental,
but I want the best for my son. The trooth.
Dis pootball, dis rugby? when he will be playing Kabbadi,
wearing only jockstrap, muscles in baby oil
with his cousins in Southall park.
Dis 'Choosing a partner' in discussions?
It's corrupting when wee will be having correct marriages.
Vut is all dis
when we will be wanting a job et di end ob da day?
Call yourself a Form Tutor, a Teacher?

Well, if he's too busy flexing his biceps, I tell you what,
I will always be a plough-pulling Punjabi,
temporarily, I am a machine operator
at the Bison concrete factory
so I want my Jaskuswinder,
that's right - Jaskuswinder, not Jackie or Jazzy or Johnny!
anyway - I want him to be sumvun:
He's doing sit ups, press ups and squats every night
then I have him chasing chickens in the bathroom.
Now I will pay for extra pudding at lunch time
if you can give him body building!
And one more ting;
why is he wid a Somali boy
doing French
wid only girls in da group?"

CULTURE CLASH

"I remember my daughter-in-law, a beaver
under the purdah, unblistered, *chappal*-less feet
run fast over hot sand to fetch sticks for the *roti* fire
or cowed by the courtyard wall:
modesty moulding dung buns in the sun
before the syrup dries. Then I would snap the chicken
from its socket, show her how to simmer each slow muscle,
when you were back from the land
we would eat from the same cooling night. Now look at her,
ever since we flew to this country, it is so unnatural,
they say she fashionably waves the men from her Datsun Sunny
as she takes the double roads like a *bunda*
she works with; they tell me she raises a *shrubby* eye:
Come on friend, I'm letting you in!
or throws out a claw if her car is in danger.
Such lovely kohl coloured eyes,
dark hunger whose spirit has crowed her away.
Where to? Who to? Even the public whose *gup-shup*,
like a Gurdwara speaker in the village she would listen to
every early morning, know son.
But what can we do for her?
with burnt voice, late at night, she returns
from some Terminal Two to bad-blooding,
daring nowadays to blaze her eyes up at mine:
Mummy-jee, why would my husband say the children run to you only?"

Notes:
chappal: sandals
roti: chapati
bunda: man
shrubby: inebriated
gup-shup: gossip

TARIQ LATIF

UNCLE MUSTKA

Hides behind a brick wall
To surprise his son.
The wall is scrawled with
'PAKIS OUT CURRY HOUSE NF'

But this does not bother
Uncle Mustka. He has just
Returned from Lahore, Pakistan,
And he waits with delight for

His son to answer the door.
Sunlight surprises Uncle Mustka
He moves away from the wall
Stands in the sun

The warmth fills his eyes
Mouth, bones and he dreams
Of a warm blue sky spread
Over Manchester, over Lahore,

Of sunshine, that bridges East and West
Kisses his brow, his paddy fields.
In the tight of his eyes
Uncle Mustka stalks the wet

Recalls the stoop of his grandfather
Rice white as bones ...
"Dad what are you doing here
You're not due back for another week?"

LETTING GO

She gasps
Quick short gasps.
He senses her struggle
But can only witness
The air
      that burns in his lungs
The air
      that fills this room
         shrink
About her pouted lips.

Her pulse loses itself in a maze of wires.
The green screen registers a flat line.
Soon he will have to disconnect his daughter.

He hangs his face
Close to her tiny lips
Sucks at her breath, whispers

"Come with me."

And the ghost of her mixes
With the pulse of his, and they
Move to the window.

"This is the green of England
I am a stranger here,
Do you see the blue sky?

It spreads far
And is hot over my land.
I am sorry I cannot take you there
Your granny ma, granny pa, and all
Your cousins are thinking of you.

We are farmers. I wanted
To show you a field of maize,
Of sugarcanes, watermelons ...
Put to your lips the goodness
Of our land, perhaps your bones
Might have grown ...”

He pauses, warm birth fluids
Wet his eyes, he feels
The gentle tug of coil
Between his sweaty palms.
The cord breaks so easily.

THE *CHUCKY*

My grandmother straddles
Around the *chucky*. She funnels
A handful of maize into the hole

Then she turns the upper slab
Clockwise, just as her mother used to.
Sometimes she feels the grainy texture

Of her grandmother's palm, sometimes
The flexible and awkward energy
Of young eager hands. Once

Light spilt from between the slabs
Of the *chucky* and the mud dried room
Filled with the spirits of all our mothers.

Voices spoke, voices hummed, voices
Sang of lush gardens, wondrous
And rich, of undying streams

And fountains that poured clear honey.
But usually all she can see
Is her aging hand, all she can feel

Is an aching absence. My mother
Has a Philips grinder and my sister
Knows how to change the fuse.

And when they make maize *roti*
We always have it with spinach
And lots of butter. Sometimes the scents

Swivel my grandmother's elbow
Before our eyes and we recall
The story of how our mother

Ran in with dad to tell
Her mum of their plans to go to England
How the grinding stopped and the flour

Spilt and the sudden silence
Was interrupted by a gust
Which shut the door on the light.

Notes:

chucky: traditional grinding stone

roti: chapati

ASIT MAITRA

THAKURDAH

The old man I never really knew
Looks down from the picture on the wall.
His delicate cheek bones and thin lips
Belie his age and wrinkles of time.

My grandfather was an ordinary clerk
In a large office filled with files.
His pen climbed every day
Up Himalayas of paperwork.

The pen in my hand carefully writes
The history of patients and their operations.
My fingers pick up scalpel and forceps
To routinely complete a mundane task.

The old man I thought I never knew
Looks down from the picture on the wall.
Now my scalpel rests. I have picked up my pen
And mountains of files are full of my poems.

FUHLWALLAH

He sells marigolds, bright orange and red,
Neatly threaded into small garlands.
A few of these hang from his large hand
Held high like a peg on the wall.

He carries a bundle on his head
And two bags in his spare hand.
Inside hide more flowers and leaves,
Sacred offerings for a Hindu god.

He wears a black top down to his waist
Matched by the dhoti, clean and white.
Brown sandals protect his feet
As he trundles along the narrow paths.

He stops at a house and makes a sale,
One or two garlands and a few leaves.
No sound, no fuss, no rush or worry,
As he goes on his journey again.

Hawkers sell their wares in many ways,
Attracting buyers by loud calls and bells.
But my flower-seller sells in silence.
He sells dream-garlands and the blindest of faith.

SOUMYEN MAITRA

IDEA FOR A POEM

Drops of midnight moon
seep through the leaves,
thinning the darkness
beneath blurred trees.

Night sighs; an owl shadows its prey
as a poem blinks in hope,
stretching its wings to the horizon
in the haze.

Fireflies tune in
as dream germinates into reality.
A whisper in the lonely breeze
playfully echoes in keys:

'Let me not die just yet.
Break the door to create
me from the curfew, open your heart,
scratch a line and let me shine through.'

CHINESE TAKEAWAY

His round face on a short body
beams next to the framed samurai.
His white coat picks up the smudges.
'Chicken Chow Mien, please,' I order,
standing over the gouty bonsai.

'Dad's on a job then?
Saw him in town ...,' he asks.
'Yes, Mr Cheong,
they'll give him a bonus
at Christmas, unless
the firm goes bust,' I reply.

His cheeks twitch
under his bare eyebrows,
his eyes disappear
beneath the hooded lids.
The happy little man
looks into the tank
and throws in a bucket of chips.

I thought he was Chinese!
But Mum says he's Cantonese.
'In China, no fish and chips!' he says.
'Chinese eat bean sprouts,
and pray for Nirvana.'

I stand at the counter and count coins.
Mr Cheong sighs, watching me.
Chicken Chow Mien arrives.

He reaches into the tank, catches a few,
shakes off the extra fat
and makes into half a bag.
'For you, no money,' he says,
all his golden fillings come into view.

SRABANTI MAITRA

CONSTELLATION

I

Tall poppies grow beside the stile by night,
some partly hidden by the hedge,
some that brush the upper rail
are rooted at the very edge.
In June of every year they come,
red or orange-tipped and tinted brown,
and touch your hands as you step down.
Sweet dreaming girls, they never learn
that men can be brutish and cruel,
so every year they come again
and some are trampled with determined zeal.

II

The night is fine and dry
with a million opposites that for a spell
look like a million souls - and soon there's none.
Then, in what seems a long time, it's gone.
Then it spins: what better than to string out
over the infinite dead spaces
the ancient beasts and spear-men of the human mind.
And if not the ancient ones, then the new.

After the wave of pain, you will turn to her
and, in an instant, change the universe to a sky
you were glad you came outside to see.
This is the act of all the descended gods
of every age and creed, too weary of all that never ends
to take a human hand and go back inside.

But try pointing them out to one you love -
you will find it quite impossible,
but like her the more for thinking
she has seen that constellation.

ROOHI MAJID

THE WEDDING

A feast of sights, smells, sounds.
The bride in her finery exudes majesty.
She is adorned in emeralds, rubies, gold;
Dressed in the finest silks and brocades,
To match the fire and the fertility rites.

Red - colour of passion and vital force;
Gold - light and warmth bearing life;
Green - the essence of nature,
Happiness and the harmony of hearts.

Her transparent veil of crimson chiffon
Has shimmering stars that dance on woven
Beams of pomegranate sheen.

A gossamer sheet hangs between,
A two-way mirror that reflects expectancy
Of gaze, heat, glow of emotion,
Bathed in musk, rose and henna.

Vermilion-sprinkling on hair-parting
Establishes marital privileges.
As the groom manages a glance,
Lashes lower and emotions are sealed.
Two hearts beat in intimacy.

An auspicious dot radiates on her forehead,
The wisdom-eye tenderly awakens while
Invisible fingers pick the sacred thread entwining
The past-present into the present-future.

KHURRAM

I named you after
a Mughal prince.
Your personality befits it.
Your passion matches
the legendary love
that lives forever
in the echoes of the Taj Mahal
that Shahjahan built
for Mumtaz Mahal.

Your eyes change
when you look at me.
Their warm mellow
gaze drips honey,
a serene blue vastness
tapers to a red flame
and a black dot quivers,
emitting sparks -
dancing stars
in pools of calmness.
I am drowned!

Your body flung at my feet,
my toes are licked wet.
Your downy chin is raised for a caress.
I love the way you place it
in the cup of my hand -
total trust, unambiguous,
unconditional.

Tail curled in, retracted claws,
your satin touch
of pearly pink paws
offers the privilege of stroking
your velvet belly!

The contour of your face
is a silent witness of devotion.
Your soft breath rising-falling
is a murmuring breeze
whispering that which
I know too well.

Inside your furry shell
you transform into
a composite purr -
alive, content - Khurram.

Note:
Khurram: The princely name of the emperor Shahjahan.

ANJUM MALIK

ALL ALRIGHT

Before the rains came, I had some hope.
Before the rains came, I had some hope.

Before the rains came, I had some hope
That it was all a hoax,
That it was all part of some big plot,
That my father was part of this big plot,
He had to appear to be dead,
He had to appear to have died,

But really he was alright
Hidden somewhere in this world,
He was still hidden somewhere on this earth,
That as soon as he could he would tell us
That it was all all right
Like it was always alright with him around,
That it was something he could not avoid

But then, when the time was right
He would come out, out of his hiding place
Working for some big undercover plot
And tell us, *sorry, but now it's all alright.*

Before the rains came, I still had some hope
I dreamed, I fantasised of this plot
Where my father had pretended to die.
It was all very hush hush and serious.

He couldn't tell us why but he was alright
And soon everything would be alright.
I dreamed and I still had some hope...

Before the rains came, late in September,
I kept dreaming of my Dad lying in a coffin,
The coffin sitting in the middle of our lounge,
My Dad lying there in his majestic form.
Suddenly he sits up laughing, *I was only kidding*, he says, laughing.
We all go quiet, we just stare

As he sits there and laughs.
Smiling, he says, *it's all alright.*

I didn't mean to die.
It was all a terrible mistake,
Now it's been put right.

Before the rains came, late in September,
I clutched onto some disappearing hope.
I kept dreaming, spinning fantasies.

Now the rain kept beating mercilessly
Against the windows, against the ground.
The rain kept coming down
Soaking, running right into the ground
Where my very own father lay
Getting wet in the ground.

SAMIA MALIK

COLOUR OF HER HEART

It's not the colour of her heart
It's the colour of her face
It's not the whisper of her dreams
It's the roar of her race...
So hard to give so hard to take
These words of love
These words of hate
Words can free her
Words can keep her in her place
What must be wrong cannot be right
No shades of grey just black and white
Words may heal you
She may die in their embrace

DIVYA MATHUR

WAVES AND THE BANK

My gift to you,
my beloved,
is the horizon itself.

I constantly search
to bring you
crystals and pearls.

Your gift to me
is always the same,
a part of yourself:
a little sand.

IRFAN MERCHANT

CROSSING

A traveller, returned from India,
may speak of mystery; of fire-walkers,
dark temples, snake-charmers, nail-beds, fakirs,
or this: a holy man on pilgrimage.

Nothing but a bowl and a stick scratching the dust.
Over his leathered skin a thin *dhoti.*
His hair and beard one splendid dirty mane.
And each step, nearing reincarnation.

A hand gesture, more ritual than signal,
as if prayer could halt the River Krishna,
the traffic parts –

buses, bicycles, taxis, trucks, rickshaws
cannot harm him,
halted by his enlightened wave.

Note:

dhoti: cloth worn around the waist and legs by Indian men

TABLEAU

My father is always standing on the deck
of the Bombay-England ship in '63,
looking back at his wife-to-be
since they were both 7,
arranged in a silk sari.

She waves farewell, then moves
to a thatched bungalow
amongst the palms of Juhu beach;
another life swinging on the verandah
seat with her books and
three children grow in the garden.

The ship docks in Tilbury
Suitcases unpack days in college
and nights in Soho lodgings,
waking with the woman
at the Gateway to India.

I'M A RACIST

If this is a paki, a darkie and a chinky, you're a racist.
    *- slogan on a poster produced by the City of
    Edinburgh Council, with three appropriate
    head-and-shoulder photos.*

I saw a paki
on the side of a bus.

I'm a paki.

I thought to myself:

How nice. A paki
on the side of a bus.

NAEEM MIRZA

FAILURE HAUNTS ME

Failure haunts me.
I live in a society
and in a time
where I have no identity.
I am considered an incomplete woman.

I am not complete
because I cannot bear children.
My marriage has failed,
I have failed my partner,
I have failed myself.
He finally gave in to the pressure
of our society and our time;
he finally deserted me.
I gave my blessings
for him to go elsewhere.
Although I accept my fate,
this is pretence.
I do not like it.

SHABNAM MUJAVER

ALONE

The grip on his bent spoon tightens,
His pale skin stretching to reveal the knotted bone beneath.
Eyes fixed on the soup as it shivers,
Awaiting its arrival to his mouth.

He rises from the chair, gripping the table in agony.
Facing the mirror he looks into the eyes of a stranger
To see a bleeding heart sigh.
His eyes lower to hinder heavy tears.
His head jerks as he remembers ...
Happy memories still haunt him.

Placing a hand to his quivering lip
He stares into the empty room.
His ears pound as he listens to the thundering silence.
Head low, a tear trickles to his chin,
As he realises his only companion is
Loneliness.

TRILOKESH MUKHERJEE

I REMEMBER

Of course I remember. Can I help it, ever?
I remember the dark blue and green world of Assam
with its strange noises, imagined creepy monsters,
the sour fruit, the betel nuts, the trickling blood of the
sacrificed goat and the marigold flowers
that I received respectfully from the priest
who touched my head as I smiled nervously behind
at the venerable savant grandfather,
a strict vegetarian but religiously dutiful.

I remember seeing the Howrah Bridge for the first time:
greyish mountain peaks against the misty sky;
the crowd, the vehicles, the piled heap of green coconuts,
the tinkling of the trams and occasional sparks.
Calcutta remains my home. I left it forty years ago,
my parents, the teachers, but most of all my friends
who made and formed me as I am today and always will be.
Please, I don't wish to know that it has changed!
I don't want to know that I too have changed.

I remember being able to say I am an Indian,
without knowing what it really meant, and
without knowing much about India. Now I hesitate.
It is a big place of many faces. I suppose I too am one of them,
and no one will miss me when that face disappears
for millions will happily take my place.
Yet I get excited when India wins the test match
and for Mother Theresa, Rushdie and for Ray.
I lower my head in shame when she explodes bombs.

I still remember when there was India, only India.
I am old now, I can't distinguish between the Pakistanis,
Bangladeshis and Indians - they are the same to me.
It may not be politically correct, I know, but then I am not.
What politics have done to us, let God, if you are there, undo,
so that we can once more breathe freely the ancient culture
of that wonderful continent: complex, colourful, moving, changing.
For I remember it not so much as a country, or even a nation,
but as an unstoppable experience, a life - at once real and dreamlike.

I am glad that I can remember. Memory is all I can now ever have.

YES, YES, MEMORIES...

Romantic or realist, young or old, lover or not,
the sun sets beyond the hazy coconut trees,
leaving a fading glowing orange halo
criss-crossed by the flying crows and stray bats.
Incense smells and smoke fill the coolish air,
conchshells and brassbells ring, from home to home,
freshly bathed mothers with bright vermilion spots on foreheads
wear freshly washed white sarees with red borders,
and bring brassplates with freshly picked jasmines
to bow down before the deities, their wet eyes glisten
in the shimmering light of the flame, as they stare
at their silent gods and pray for their children,
never ever for themselves, and heaven only knows
that they need it more really, just to see a glimmer of light
at the end of the tunnel of daily domestic life.

And us children?
We listened to the untiring chirping of crickets and nightjars,
the hooting of the nightowls and the howling of distant jackals,
the glowworms added golden firework sparks on the dark canvas,
smelled the smoke of the fire and the food being cooked,
the smell of the rice boiled over the hot earthen oven....
Much later, after the meal shared with all the children,
lying down on the cool straw mats in the dark, listening to the stories
Grandmother told, her reassuring voice transported us
to another far away unknown, yet familiar, world;
the stories heard again and again, yet never quite satisfying.
"...And then, Grandma! What happened then?" We all knew,
but wanted to hear it again from Grandma's lips, the stories of
sad Damayanti, valiant Bheema, wonderful Bishma, Krishna -
we never knew when we fell asleep with wet eyelids
for the dreamworld was not much different either,
except that there we met the heroes and heroines
and spoke to them and played with them.

Grandmother is no more. But the dreams are still with us.
I can still hear her voice and feel her presence.
I need only shut my eyes to hear the whispering,
to feel the presence of the stories and our lost lives.

That's what the memories are about.

RAMAN MUNDAIR

AN ELEGY FOR TWO BOYS

I

Ruptured concrete suburban skin holds
taut the poison that is paved within
feet are sweet against the sting.
You're cushioned so (u)l/e up
the cartography of the metropolis
A-Z veins re-route via fingertips clutch
Have travel card will travel...
zones 1-6.
The world is your oyster
but London killed you.

II

It was like any other day.
Nothing unusual, just the same:
walking to the bus-stop/ walking into town...
After a while it's a blur
kingstonelthamkingstonelthamkingstoneltham
just the same, nothing unusual
just the same, nothing unusual.
It was my mate who saw them,
he said RUN!
I said no, we haven't done anything wrong.

III

Their unavoidable existence
internal morsic heartbeat screams; FLIGHT!
trained feet seize up in a fit of dignified pride
thoughts like 'but they're as human as me'
translate into reasoning syntax that escapes like gas
into the dense onyx sky and zeroes
into the void between their eyes.
A breath later
you are running like the hunted,
a breath later

you are kissing blood into water,
a breath later
you are kissing blood into concrete.

IV

When it comes it's not like the movies
when it comes it's like a joke.
But you're not laughing, can't believe
that it's really happening, for real, you know?
And I didn't see my life flash in front of my eyes.
I just heard my mother's voice
'Ricky, *Beta... Tu kider gay-a? Mai karh tinu ureekdi hai....*'
I just heard my dad's voice
'Stephen, son... Where you go? Me still waiting at the door for you to come home....'

Note:
Beta... Tu kider gay-a? Mai karh tinu ureedkdi hai...
Son, where did you go? I was waiting for you.

OSMOSIS

Memories
Of safety,
Oneness.

My mother,
Cross-legged on the floor,
A *parât* of fresh *methé*
In front of her.

Me,
Small and slithery enough
To squeeze
Through the hook
Of her
Working arms
And fingers
Plucking succulent leaves
From the stem.

My head
Resting on her shalwared thighs,
Feeling warmth
Oozing through her
Skin to skin
Osmosis
Safety.

Watching sweet, fragrant *methé*
Fall like angels
Into the *parât*,
Knowing that soon
There will be
Fresh *parathé* with *methé* inside
And ghee melting
Into it's crevices
With homemade *dhai*
In small metal bowls
With indentations like steel musical drums.

Feelings content
Stirrings,
Nestlings.
Turning my face towards
Her special place,
The one where the greatest warmth
Glows.
Where one scent roots me
And leaves me with desires
Of burying myself deep inside.

Awakenings with connections
Of my hands
Coyly identifying my own special place.
"What are you doing?"
My mother's hands stop,
Her eyes fix on mine
"*Ki kar di hai*?"
My hand wavers and works it's way back up.
I say calmly and clearly
"It feels good, Mamma, it feels real nice
When I touch myself here."

I watch her face.
She does not falter.
Her face fills with warm colour,
Her mouth widens.
She eases me off her *godi*
And, smiling, says
"You naughty girl,
Go and play."

Notes:

parât: container

methé: fenugreek

parathé: folded and fried chapati or pancake

dhai: curds

"*Ki kar di hai*?": "What are you doing?"

godi: lap

MAYA NAIDOO

AMA

Ama
swollen
and laden
with syrupy
Natal heat. Sturdy
and roaring with blunt
determination. Carrying
in a land not of her lineage
my father's generation
jostling against her fleshfield.

Lakshmi, Latchmamma, Almalammah
no-one knows precisely which or why three names
honouring godly Fortune and winding Telegu tongues.
Latchmamma, Almalammah, conjuring Mother India
Dravidian land unsmelt by Ama, unseen. Born of people shipped
by a sweet-toothed empire.

Groaning forth into South Africa's year-round sugar slopes
nine babies burnished biscuit-brown. Honeyed infants honed
by whispering cane, leaves like swords splicing sky. Her wailing nine
and then three more, bedded in bite-size coffins, half-memoried
murmurs in the dreams of my generation.

Grandchildren, calling her Ama like our own mother.
Familiar with her cradling roses, squinting in sepia; brushed up and
                                                            lamp lit
before we might hang from her sari, learning the nuance of her tongue.
Before our Age of Dispersal over a map once candy-floss pink.

Lakshmi, tucked within my own three names.
England-born, bloodlines trailing continents like molasses.
Sitting in this not-of-my-Mother country I retell myself
Ama's story from fragments heard and chew cane
tired from my suitcase. My long journey
I squeeze dry fibres for juice
with my sweet tooth.

SUNITI NAMJOSHI

THE DWARFS

Disabled doesn't mean disqualified, or perhaps it does?

i)

        Snow White sleeps
and the dwarfs go crazy, scrabbl-
           ing in the dark
for the means of life.
        They cannot covet her.
(It is not permitted.)
        But possibly they love her.
What can she offer?
        Possibly her presence,
perfuming their days
        with light and love?
Look, but don't touch!
Wistful children
        peer through the pane.
Who is their keeper?
        And what the secret?
When Snow White wakes,
    who smashes open
        their house of glass?

ii)

        Later, no bitter lies, though dwarfs
          may offer a silent surprise.
          My name was Cordelia.
       Though the mirror erased me,
          my mother loved me
          when I was very small.

iii)

My name was Stout Heart!
              Mine Courage!
      But our third sister
      - no, do not laugh -
she was the bravest of us all.
The bad queen thought her ugly.
The good queen thought her mad.
                  But the mirror
stopped its smirking,
              grew thoughtful and sad.

iv)

Yes, I was bashful -
not first in the scuffle,
not first in the race -
both Backward and Bashful.
                  How explain?
I felt no lack, no loss of grace.

v)

              And I wasn't sleepy, I was asleep.
              My brothers didn't mind.
              My sisters tended me.
      When I woke up I told my dream.
      They cried: manna! roses!
              lilies! ice-cream!
              whatever was,
              or might have been.

vi)

              Last but not least, I was Beautiful.
              Oh do not smile a reticent smile.
      My name was Snow White, Sister, Dwarf.
      Now no bitterness, no needless guile.

AMONG TIGERS

Must live among tigers, but can take time off
when the tigers are busy or have fed enough
to admire their prowess, their muscular grace,
the easy assurance of a lordly race.
From their point of view I exist, of course,
but am hardly central, a fact of sorts,
and of no consequence to their magnificence ...

To bait a tiger - a fearful boast:
but given their 'norms', their manners and laws
such a deed would elicit no applause.
And yet, it might be worth it - almost -
to observe in action a tiger's reaction.

You see, I have survived so long,
my habit of observation grown so strong
that sometimes I think I almost belong.
I know exactly how a tiger drinks,
how a tiger walks, smiles and thinks,
but find somehow that I cannot ape
that unthinking pride or its manifest shape.
I fully understand the Tigrish Cause
and keep my distance from those massive jaws.

IN THAT PARTICULAR TEMPLE

In that particular temple
        a god slept
and a goddess danced,
            and in another
a goddess slept and a god
            danced.
Do I dare say it? Perhaps -
        it is possible -
that it's all the same?
        That rapt
and dispassionate stare,
        the flaring curve
of the gorgeous hip
         and the round
and unashamed breasts,
         I have worshipped
before. When we make love
        you and I
are both sacred and secular.
        The goddess's limbs
begin to move.
         Balanced underfoot
the world spins.

NAZRUL ISLAM NAZ

THE ROARING SILENCE

Of all the languages in this world
Silence
Is the most powerful,
And you, my dear,
Have mastered it.
What you say
Keeps me in ecstasy,
What you decide
Not to say
Kills me.

FRIDAY, 6TH OF MARCH, 1998

Just say
for the sake of saying
if you and I were talking,
we would say,
in remembering the other night:
"It was a night to remember."
Since we don't

have that chance
all too often
to come together
and talk,
I decided
on our behalf
to keep a record
by way of
say, a simple poem
where I won't labour
over rhyme or metre,
but write a few
short

simple
sentences
just like the meeting
we had.
No big deal, no big subject.
A few laughs, a few reflections
here and there,
as they come quite naturally.

In that cafe
we didn't eat much,
but what we had
was sufficient.

It so happens,
once in a long while,
that thoughts of food
are forsaken
for the sole desire
of companionship.

MICHAEL NAZIR-ALI

'HAIKU' - HOLY WEEK 1995

Malling Abbey sits
Prayers to absorb
And give back - God.

Benedict rules OK
Where Gundulph has built
There lives are remade.

TRINITY SUNDAY AT KWANGJU

In two rooms above a welder's shop,
I saw the Lord high and lifted up
at Kwangju!

Tailor, smith and watch-maker were gathered there,
I saw the Lord high and lifted up
at Kwangju!

The Temple of the Lord! The Temple of the Lord!
I saw the Lord high and lifted up
at Kwangju!

A grimy staircase was Jacob's ladder for me,
I saw the Lord high and lifted up
at Kwangju!

No room for him in Bethlehem, but here there was,
I saw the Lord high and lifted up
at Kwangju!

A darkish corner for the Body and the Blood,
I saw the Lord high and lifted up
at Kwangju!

The young man angry at his own weakness,
I saw the Lord high and lifted up
at Kwangju!

The young women imagining they were single mothers,
  I saw the Lord high and lifted up
    at Kwangju!

Their hidden Lord they wanted out in shop and street,
  I saw the Lord high and lifted up
    at Kwangju!

"When I am lifted up, I will draw you to myself", he said,
  I saw the Lord high and lifted up
    at Kwangju!

An upper room there was, no Pentecost yet,
  I saw the Lord high and lifted up
    at Kwangju!

Transfigured for you may they come down,
  those humble folk of yours
    at Kwangju!

Note:

The Old Testament reading for Trinity Sunday is from *Isaiah* 6: 1-8. It is about the prophet's vision of God "high and lifted up". Kwangju in South-West Korea is a traditionally poor part of the country. It is a city with a reputation for dissent from the repressive policies of successive regimes.

NARANJAN SINGH NOOR

DUNKIRK!

Can Darwin's 'evolution' be reversed, Plato?
Monkeying with the question
for a few light moments,
the philosopher grabbed hold of a latest computer
with its ultimate software
and retreated in reverse gear
to the jungle of civilization.
What an honourable retreat!

HUGO SALEEL NURBHAI

CONSPIRACY THEORY

1) Caleb thought
he was being pursued
by:
the Knights Templar, the Masons, the Rosicrucians,
the Heralds of the Golden Dawn;
Crowleyists, Cabalists, Masters of Tibet;
and the Elders of Zion - or Sion.

Of course he wasn't,
was he.

2) Caleb thought
he was being pursued
by:
the Knights Templar, the Masons, the Rosicrucians,
the Heralds of the Golden Dawn;
Crowleyists, Cabalists, Masters of Tibet;
and the Elders of Zion - or Sion.

Of course he wasn't.
...Was he?

AN AFFAIR OF THE HEART

I knew two people once.
One had a husband, one had a wife.
But they had an affair.
Together.

No-one could know.
So - what they did was this:

whenever they met, each would go,
each and on their own,
at different times
to different tables
at different pubs or restaurants.

When sleeping together, each would go,
each and on their own,
on different nights
to different beds
in different hotels in distant towns.

It was brilliant - it worked;
and no one suspected a thing

They took it even further.
They would holiday together.

But, so no-one would know,
they went each and on their own
on different planes
to different places
at different times of year.

But how did they enjoy themselves?
What did they do
if they wanted to have
the odd spot of belly-slapping?

Silly question; silly me.
I could answer myself
immediately.

They did not need to meet:
their souls were joined
spiritually.

No, they were not.
They liked a bunk-up now and then.
But to avoid being found out,
instead of with the lover,
each would leap into bed with the respective spouse.

It was foolproof -
this most secret
of secret liaisons.
No-one had known
that anything furtive
had ever gone on.

But ...
things like this must always end.
And ...

one evening, completely by chance,
the respective spouses went
each and on their own
on different nights
to different tables
at different pubs -
and didn't find them there.

So they were forced to end the whole affair.

KAUSER PARVEEN

DANGEROUS EXCITEMENT

You were the dangerous excitement
my father, my family, warned me about.
You were the distant forbidden fruit
        I could not taste
- under any circumstances.

Then I suddenly grew.
I suddenly turned
from child to woman,
without the knowledge,
without the consent
        of anyone.
I had achieved something
for which I could not gain a certificate,
could not be given accreditation.

The dangerous excitement
I was warned about
        loomed nearer:
dangerous, exciting.

YOGESH PATEL

THE VALUES

I bottled the Ganges
and set sail
in quest of Re.
On the banks of the Nile
with Mokele of Lake Tumba
and Nkombe, the Mongo warrior,
I shared the hookah
while, for the bottled Ganges,
I elevated a temple.
Mokele stole the sun,
Nkombe opened God's gift on the horizon;
they danced as the first light came:
"the sun's found, the sun's found!"
But then they came in their army uniforms
and, alas! We were kicked out,
the bottled Ganges and I.

On the shores where Canute once sat,
I tried to wash off my sin:
my greatest crime, my skin.

I wash not with Canute's waters,
I wash not with bottled Ganges,
But in the devil's dream
I'm doomed to do so in rivers of blood.

I refuse to be consumed.
A skinhead throws a stone at me
to smash the Ganges bottle.
I run, run, and run -
like a rat in a subterranean castle,
I still carry the burden of this bottle!
I dilute it with tap water
and lo! I drink it!
In the communion, I dilute it more
and share, and share...
The Ganges, unleashed like a genius,
swells and swells, and knows no bounds.

Such arrogance! It mocks it's own mother!

Engulfed, I look for my name
at Thoth's Heliopolis, the mound at Khemenu,
in Ayodhya, Kurukshetra and Ashoka's Kalinga,
in the streets of Brixton and Tottenham.
Alas! I am nothing but the bloody skin...

The skin is a passport,
the skin is a number.
The passport's tattooed with a number;
the number, the essence, has no flesh, no bones.
With such legacy, I tell my son, "I'm waiting -
I'm waiting for Prajapati to utter,
'*BHUR*', so I can find the earth,
'*BHUVAH*', so I can find the air,
and '*SVAH*', so I can have the sky.
Then I can begin:
I can give you hope,
the plain for the sun to rise above
and the Ganges to come down...

Until then, this is it,
hang it around your neck -
THIS BOTTLED GANGES!"

Notes:

Re: Ancient Egyptian sun god.

Mokele: An African folkloric hero, born from his mother's cosmic egg, who steals the sun in order to give life.

Nkombe: A legendary warrior from African folklore.

Thoth's Heliopolis: Thot was the ancient Egyptian god who invented letters, arts and sciences. Heliopolis was the centre of the cult of Re in ancient Egypt.

The mound at Khemenu: The centre of the cult of Thot.

Ayodhya: An Indian town, famous as the birthplace of Rama and, in recent years, as a place of conflict between Hindus and Muslims.

Kurukshetra: An Indian town, famous as the battlefield in the *Mahabharata* epic.

Ashoka's Kalinga: When he saw the carnage at the battlefield of Kalinga, the Indian emperor, Ashoka, decided to renounce war and embrace Buddhism.

Prajapati: Lord of all living things, another name for Brahma the Creator in Hindu belief.

BHUR BHUVAH SVAH: Part of the opening line of the famous Gayatri mantra in Sanskrit.

TYPICAL MR PATEL'S TYPICAL PROMOTION

Mr Patel, you're blah blah blah.
BUT...
Can you fill in this form - for equal opportunity?
It's to allow us to monitor you-know-what.
Thank you. We'll let you know in due course.
(Never.)

Mr Patel,
Sorry.

You were one of the two selected,
BUT...
(Hell, you smell of *masala*.)
Try again next year.
(And the year after, and after, and after...)
Thank you for your interest in our company.

The calf butted the oak:
Mr Patel bought the company
and promoted himself.

Note:
masala: spices

KAILASH PURI

CIRCLE LINE

I like the Circle Line:
whichever way it goes
the destination is always mine.
Life is like that:
at one end is the cat, at the other the rat.
There is no waiting,
both give a lesson
in patience without dating.
In the Circle Line
one has only to sit
like someone stupid -
without wisdom or wit -
like a cupid
whose arrows need not hit.
You may kiss a blonde,
you may make or break a bond,
or sit alone, just moan and groan,
you may read, do a good deed,
go to sleep, sneak or peep
or do nothing -
just act like a stone.
You will never miss
for the train will bring you
time and again
to your station.
The Circle Line is God's plan,
made alike for the crow and the swan.
But alas! I missed it
even though I ran.

KARMA

The lawn of my heart
Is filled with weeds,
The fountain of my life
Is studded with reeds.
Where do I plant
These remaining seeds
Of borrowed days?
How can I hide
The naked deeds
That I have committed?
How can I hide
From the just eyes
That usher in Summer
In early June
Or bring in a wintry moon
Towards the end of a cycle?
Before mid noon
They came like locusts
In a swarm
And devoured the remaining
Blades of green.
They came like bees
And sucked
The last drop of nectar
From the last flower.
Acting methodically,
And in haste,
They converted my heart
Into a waste,
Though once so green and warm.

PADMAJA RAO

FOR YOU

Your memory beats inside me.
No songs, just blind thumps against
half-painted ribcage. Every morning
my front door chokes on bills,
unsolicited letters. My toes curl inside
my shoes as I wait for blue leaves
to rain. Sister, we are caught
up in a ritual. We plant bulbs
in strange lands and hope they'll
last the winter. Soon, I'll have
tea in my glass house and watch
the autumn grass grow slowly.
But how do I weed the distance?

THE JOURNEY

We crawl out of Delhi
dotted with the faded beads
of paraffin lamps;
the sky splattered with red.
Hungry men
desperate to get home.
Our carriage rolls into
the tunnels to the cryptic chants
of strange pilgrims.
We share the same journey
but different destinations.
Together we surrender
to the night of *Malkauns*.

Well beyond the dark realms
of sleepy English villages
is a piece of land and
a buried soul
shielded by stiff, cold wreaths.
Lips of petals make lullabies
and the snow crumbles down
to the rhythm.
My arms feel
emptier
than the barren country road
which slips further from the prayers
as we grope deeper into the forest.

The night churns the hours;
a milky haze
fluffs around us.
Headless trees
each one a soldier
watches as the
fog of Kashmir engulfs us.

Note:

   Malkauns: a serious and peaceful classical raga which is played only at night.

IAN IQBAL RASHID

ANOTHER COUNTRY

All this new love of my parents' countries. We have bought the videotapes together, bought the magazines and books, all the advertisements, clothes, and each others' responses. We watch the slides of your visit. Your handsome face is tanned surrounded by mango trees, planted above the poverty. The moist beauty - which you think of blowing up and then framing, building into your walls - majesty imposed upon majesty.

Now I watch you watch Sergeant Merrick watch poor Hari Kumar. And follow as the white man's desire is twisted, manipulated into a brutal beating. You are affected by the actor's brown sweating body, supple under punishment. What moves you? The pain within the geometry of the body bent? The dignity willed in the motions of refusal? A private fantasy promised, exploding within every bead of sweat? Or is it the knowledge of later: how my body will become supple for you, will curve and bow to your wishes as yours can never quite bend to mine. What moves you then?

My beauty is branded into the colour of my skin, my strands of hair thick as snakes, damp with the lushness of all the tropics. My humble penis cheated by the imperial wealth of yours: Hari's corporal punishment, mine corporeal. Yet this is also part of my desire. Even stroking myself against your absence, I close my eyes and think of England.

RETURNING TO CANADA

I arrive again, my returns timed like coincidences. Immediately, I cock my kindness like knobby wings, and cluck too much.

All day your house is dark, drapes closed. A crack of light cuts through the velvet feeling, transforms the dust in the air into a sparkling chandelier. And the house is full of visitors - they sit quiet in chairs at appalled angles to each other. Every now and again, we rise suddenly, cup your few words like raindrops in a drought.

Your white face becomes shadowed by a violet colour of night under your eyes and I put you to sleep. I am waiting to remove my clown's smile, muscles tired from all the faces I have made. The only sounds now are an occasional rattle: my tired natter and the bottles half-filled with pills that I feed you - bottles with choppy, energetic names on them like sounds from another language.

Downstairs, I finally think I hear you sleeping, my every tendon tense between each of your long slow breaths. I imagine a rectangle cutting through the ceiling, your stark bones lying perpendicular to the beams of the attic.

I still feel this thing for you - a longing that causes my insides to lurch as if I had leaned out over a cliff. I wake up trying to remember, knowing I have dreamed some possibility that I had never before considered.

SELINA RODRIGUES

MISSING

Princess Diana is alive and well
I've seen her, in Agra.

She sips water from an aluminium cup
plays with the sunlight on the opposite wall
wears her kameez and dupatta
modestly now, with jeans.

Like me she has come here for the second time
against her wildest dreams.
She misses only a certain coolness
She checks-in visitors, to air-conditioned rooms.

Photos of her flock the walls of the world.
Missing, have you seen this woman?
Wept for this person as I have?
Just tell her that we love her.

Don't worry, she is safe with Mumtaz
whom she lifts from the tomb at night.
She laughs at pigeon shit on the marble
leaves a thumbprint.

Skirts camcorders, slowly loses herself
in the audience, of the filmy eternal Taj.

MUSEUM

I find my background in day trips.
My multi-coloured parents
in the mono-coloured sixties
struggling in the colour prison
learnt to ignore their past.
So I practise for travel.

There is a great arc of white.
People wrestle with plans
unmanageable as sails.
I learn that Europeans learnt glass
from the East. Teasing with their breath
the beauty of perfect joining.

It all feels very beautiful
the coolness, the cabinets of preservation.
You know, in a way, we come very willingly
we come to see our belongings
we come to visit the stolen goods.
Do not touch. Get a postcard.

I remember when the carpet lay to the ground,
red so deep it took a beat with each step.
Sweat poured as I sliced the tile
my lifeline running with blood and water.
I balance with stone cold under my hands in the shade
heat beneath my feet in the sun.

I place my postcard in my house
next to my dad's car boot brass lamp
my mum's dolphin mobile.
After the divorce they each go shopping
and I take what they didn't want from each other.
Eagerly, as if they are presents.

SAIQAH SALIM

YOU TAKE ME

You take me for granted.
You think you own me.
You think you have a right over me.
You think you can physically abuse me, scar me.
You take me for granted.
You tell me what to do,
Tell me how to do it,
Tell me when to do it.
You take me for granted.
You tell me I'm no good,
Tell me I'm useless,
Tell me I'm worthless.
You abuse my love,
Abuse my body,
Abuse my mind.
You take me for granted.
How long
Until I'm gone?

ASHOKA SEN

MY ENDING IS LIKE MY BEGINNING

At the beginning it was all chaotic
inconsequential and disconnected.
It was like the pieces of a jigsaw-puzzle
jumbled up
and scattered all over the place.
I started to pick and arrange them
matching and inter-locking,
joining one with another.

My child eyes detected all the hidden clues
and in no time at all a picture
meaningful and coherent
started to take shape.
The mosaic floor under my feet
with its distinctive floral pattern
came into my view.
I learnt who I was
and where I was.
I explored all the links
that joined me with others
on the mural painting.
The connecting fluid
that bound us together
on the panoramic frame
was love.

I am well away from my beginning now
but things are still in fragments,
the tapestry is not yet complete,
some of the pieces of the jigsaw-puzzle
are still missing.
The connecting fluid within me
is drying out fast.
I cannot join things with things any more.
The passion I brewed within my heart
is all spent up.
My ending is like my beginning:
the picture is getting smudged and blurred
looking more and more chaotic.

THE PAST LIKE THE CHORUS CHARACTER

When all the voices outside go quiet at night,
the past rises.
Like the chorus character of a Greek play,
it starts telling and interpreting the events
of our-yesterday,
linking them to the present.

Have you heard the voice
ringing within your head in the lonely hours?
Do you like it?
Or do you find it too disturbing?
Do you want to turn it off and focus the light
on the chorus girls instead?
- the dream girls leading to the future,
repeating the same refrain
again and again and again,
dulling and blocking your brain
with a mesmeric rhythm?

The voice of the chorus past is drowned.
The midnight music is too loud.
The only hope you pinpoint
is the chorus girls
who, with their hypnotic voices, will lead the way
to the rostrum of the future.

SATI SEN

MY DEAR FRIEND

I am made of stone in the form of a statue.
An excellent work of a sculptor,
Credit goes to my creator.
People look at my erotic figure,
They appreciate its artistic beauty,
But I have my own feelings
That nobody wants to know.
I am free, a young girl, spending time with flowers.
Birds and rabbits are my friends;
I cannot stand the noise of people -
They are not my type.
That's why I like to be on my own
And wander in the green garden.
Accidentally I bumped into a statue
And was startled to see it looking at me.
I exclaimed: "What a beautiful creature you are,
My dear friend!"

STONE

A stone:
small, smooth, oval shaped,
whispered from the beach.
Who knows its beginning?
          she thought.
It's very precious,
put it under a pillow.

That night she had a dream.
'Do you know my story?'
asked a tiny voice from the pillow.
'Mount Everest is my father.
I escaped quietly down the glacier.
She dropped me at
the source of Gangotri
where the River Ganges begins to flow.
She asked me to follow.

I passed the gorges and
came towards the land.
All through the journey
I am flowing and rolling -
I found life,
I am no longer a dead stone.
I can no longer hold back
the force of life and the force of joy.
I hear the ocean's call -
I cannot be held.'

SUDEEP SEN

FLYING HOME

I meticulously stitch time through the embroidered sky,
  through its unpredictable lumps and hollows. I

am going home once again from another
  home, escaping the weave of reality into another

one, one that gently reminds and stalls
  to confirm: my body is the step-son of my soul.

But what talk of soul and skin
  in this day and age, such ephemeral things,

that cross-weaves blood and breath
  into clotted zones of true escape.

What talk of flight time and flying
  when real flights of fancy are crying

to stay buoyant unpredictably in mid-air
  amid pain, peace, and belief: just like thin air

sketches, where another home is built
  in free space vacuum, as another patchwork quilt

is quietly wrapped around, gently, in memoriam.

TRANSLATING POETRY

Your poem translated itself so many times:
   From the incipient thoughts that brewed
   in your mind, as your mother tongue fumed
straining to come together, trying

to emerge from shapelessness
   to a semblance of shape. Re-piecing
   together the shattered mirror, remoulding
and reflecting light from unknown niches,

the poem switched tongue and its skin
as the oblique image stamped its imprint.

But the translation wasn't quite done:
   It was fed into a computer
   to be processed, polished further,
and parts re-written, then fed again. One

strange beast of an electronic transmission
   ate the poem again, the fodder waxed
   and its shape reshaped. Then out of my fax
at night, a sheet of glazed emission

emerged, words on an unsuspecting tray.
A real poem defies translation, in every way.

DADU

Three years back I held Dadu, my grandfather, through
    the second attack in the Intensive Care Unit,
surrounded by smells of doctors, dis-
    infectants, drugs, and his sweat,
as he convulsed fiercely fighting for life.

I held him all the way through,
    watching the beads of his sweat
glisten among the neon-lit
    panels, pipes, pins, graphs, glucose,
as he cried out breathlessly for life.

The dreaded moments, struggling, gasping to
    live. I was just as drenched as he was. I saw:
his eyes closed, he lay there silently with his
    heaving chest rise and fall
as all the sweat beads rolled down his sides.

He breathed back, barely, to
    yet another survival.
I was not present there, this
    time. Trying to hold him again
from ten thousand miles

away, I overheard by mail: Didu,
    my grandmother, absolutely cold, choked, pale,
spoke the only words she's spoken since:
    "All our grandchildren except you saw him,
you weren't here, to save him, this time."

SENI SENEVIRATNE

CINNAMON ROOTS

Cinnamon sweet wood spice
once traded like gold
when I look for my roots
I find you yellowish brown
like my winter skin
native of Sri Lanka
growing wild in the jungles
of the Kandy Highlands

1492 Columbus never finds you
sailing westwards to the lands
of the Arawak Indians
he promises spices and gold
trophies for a Spanish Queen
brings her Taino slaves as 'gifts'

But Portugal travels East
to an island that falls like
a teardrop from the tip of India
finds your soft sweetness
wraps it in hard cash
grows rich on your rarity
founding a spice trade
that deals in blood

The Dutch make plantations
tame your wild fragrance
that can never sweeten their breath
demand quotas of your bark
enforced by death and torture
burn down your August harvest
fabled fuel of the phoenix fire
to keep up the prices

Dutch East India
becomes British East India
your acres grow in the rain
and heat of Sri Lanka

filling the coffers
of the British Empire

1992 I buy your ground aroma
in pre-packed jars fry you
with aubergines and coriander
look for my roots
find you yellowish brown
like my winter skin
native of Sri Lanka
growing wild in the jungles
of the Kandy Highlands

LENA RULAK

Who are you Lena Rulak
mother of my father
daughter of a lawyer
Eurasian Burgher
of Sri Lanka?

You are my father's
speechless memories
moving through me
like the sea
in my restless sleep

you wrap me in his body
clothe me in words
that have wandered
through oceans
wash me up
on the dream tide

your arms are wide
and change the blue
to gold
you treasure me
in smells
of spices and kindness
cradle me
in a language

I never knew
turn my questions
into songs

JUST JEALOUS

"They're just jealous"
My mum used to say to me
When I came crying
Home from school
Saying they'd called me "nigger"
And it made sense then
Because I liked my brown skin.

But it didn't make sense
In later years
When a man drove his car
At me on a beach
Shouting "black bastard"
He wasn't "just jealous"
He was angry that I'd answered back.

Yet I can't say
She was wrong to say it
Thinking today of a black child in care
Scrubbing her skin till it bleeds
Trying to make it white
I want to say
"Didn't anyone ever tell you
That your black skin is nice
And they're all just jealous".

And when my own daughter
Comes home from school
Asking why they call her "Paki"
Shall I say "just jealous"
Or try to explain
The centuries of racism
That are heaped behind that word?

And will it make more sense
Than what my mum said to me?

KHADIJA SHAHJAHAN

TUBEROSES

Clean, pure, delicate,
A scattering of white
Against a dancing parade of green grass.
Gift of quiet happiness
To those in ill-health,
A bouquet of get-well wishes,
A survivor of cruel seasons
And trampling feet.
Lacking the colour of other flower associates,
Yet still winning over the world
With caressing fragrance and gentle air....

TASLIMA SHAHJAHAN

LONDON

Places,
Fazes,
Just like mazes,
London City business bases,
Cases,
Paces,
Commuter faces
In London city rat races.

JOHN SIDDIQUE

perfume

o with the smell of oil and flowers

with samarkand and sandalwood anoint me

bathe deep in rose water

and walk as shimmering light
dappled on the ground
                    everywhere

there must be incense
this serpent loves the smell

plait flowers for me

with betel leaf reddening your lips
kiss me
        kiss me

blues for Ambedkar

politics & religion
would have you born under wheels

the weak
the poor
the children of god
... that's the way it was made
the layers are unboundable

Ambedkar as a boy sits outside
the classroom
taking in everything
these children cannot mix they are caste and outcast

Ambedkar learnt the law
for 50 years he believes
that a new constitution is the path
to a new Maharashtra and India

the law still speaks in the static language
of its fetters

under wheels we are broken

the way to be free of the father/mother
is to grow up
to cease to be one of god's children
we must leave god
leave the human ideas of that notion

there is pain

there is a cause of pain

by pulling out the roots we shall
understand and overcome the pain

there is a path to take us through

Buddham Saranam Gacchami

Dhammam Saranam Gacchami

Sangham Saranam Gacchami

Notes:
Ambedkar: a great leader of the untouchables, he founded the neo-Buddhist movement
in India and is known as the Father of the Indian Constitution
*Buddham Saranam Gacchami / Dhammam Saranam Gacchami / Sangham Saranam
Gacchami*: I take refuge in the Buddha / I take refuge in the Dhamma / I take refuge in
the Sangha

neckgrip

after the funeral
i found a box of photos

my mum had only ever shown me
old polaroids my dad had took
and her wedding album
        full of the few
        guests & had-to-be-there's

i.e. those who kept their thoughts,
about a black marrying a white woman,
behind their own curtains

you might call it the presence of duty

there are 3 photos in the box
all of them portraits
taken at some local photographer's studio

the props of the 50's, almost victoriana
and my father in his best suit
his neck and back rigid
in one he is holding a briefcase
in another he is pictured with a radio
in the last photograph, it is just him
standing against a dark curtained background
in his sharpest clothes:
all poses of affluence to be sent home
to give the impression of success

at home i remember
my mum telling me
about having to work 12, 14 hours in the shop
and the scraps she had to make meals with

DURLABH SINGH

LADY OF MY DREAMS

Lady of my dreams
Moon-coloured
Raven-haired
Inaccessible
Like a distant shore.

Dwelling here
Closer to the heart
A reason, a dream
Undefined yet real.

Moon-coloured pebbles
Shining among plains
A cluster
Deeply driven
Etched like a wound
A rose or a moan
Or a crimson scar
A luminosity
Or a distant spark.

Lady of my heart
Moon-coloured
Raven-haired
Inaccessible
Like a distant star.

GERRY SINGH

IN MY LOVE'S EYES

I could see the hills in my love's eyes
And in her hair the moss and mirrored *lochan*

We stood awhile beneath Stob Gabhar
Warm as rocks in the morning sun

The whispering clouds lifted late
And we saw the moors return to Rannoch

As bending grasses green and yellow
Danced around each pool of blue

The path was laid and fixed with stiles
Each mile supporting bridge inviting

To be in such a place as this
Perched on a ladybird's little black dot
Or flitting in a butterfly's see-through wing
Or rising in the flight of a stonechat winging
And the ringing bells of all the birds singing
Is to know that love is the only gift
If you take it by the hand and gently drift.

Note:
lochan: a small loch or lake

LADHAR BHEINN

Little cairns mark the way like hill stations
For the independent minded.
Fifty years have passed
Since the Gandhis lived at number forty-seven.
Here, spiders do not hide in caves
Swinging away from the light
And waiting on a sign.

A colourful crowd head for the summit.

The rock stood up
Walled in a halted hardness
And all that is hidden
From the historian's little perch

Whose tiny trickle
Cannot disturb the continuing flow
Of water on stone.

The astonished stag freezes time,
His wait measured in breaths
Lost from way back then
When Bruce was bold.

Stepping in the rich chocolate peat
Travellers plod and mutter
Rinsing out the squelch of absenteeism
To welcome home to the fold
The leaky streets of Glasgow and Calcutta.

Nothing to crow about yet
While dressed up *spuggies*
Tell us tales that do not tally.

For ruler and ruled alike
The rock waits.
The path is clear,
Dry and dusty as an Asian mouth
Where colour, birth or better
Cannot fashion a sari from a fetter
Or lock horns with the king of the deer
Who waits for you to move.

Note:

spuggies: sparrows

INDIA GATE

The noon sun over Delhi
Lit up the M8.

On my soft shoulder
Was a hard shoulder
Laying out a long carpet
To the pink city of Jaipur.

Looking towards the Lomonds
I saw a lama
On the cooling heights of Simla
Walking on a cloud of dust.

And a small train
Rattling the iron gauges
Fuelling a trip to the Ganges.

Waiting on the platform
At Varanasi
I met so many strangers
Who had been here before.
Watched them
Bathing in the warm light
Where emperors had stood
Not hearing the thundering clatter
Of the Raj.

And reflected in the churned
Up waters of the flood
Was a lovely child of both.

MAHENDRA SOLANKI

AFTER A WHILE YOU BELIEVE THE LIES YOU TELL

That bump on your head -
did your father really throw you down the stairs?

- that story about your name and how,
not able to read, write or speak English
you copied the Sikh girl's name as your own -
and you say no-one noticed
until you moved to another school.

And that one about how
you said you'd care for me
and would die
rather than do any harm?

There are no pictures of you as a child,
no way of checking if that lump was there before.
There are no old exercise books with the girl's name.
There is no piece of paper with your promise -

just this ring, the words I recall and this bruise.

IN A JAR

I collect you in a jar.

I always imagined it would be ornamental,
                                                    like a trophy.
It is plastic and weighs more than
its square shape suggests.

I lower you gently into the boot of the car, you in
a plastic jar propped against plastic bags full of offerings.

I have a thud in my head *Shri Ram jaya Ram*
as dull as the brown of the jar.
Shri Ram jaya Ram jaya jaya Ram.
I am driven to discard your remains in running water.

>   *I imagine all your hardened*
>   *edges made smooth;*
>   *a life-time's harshness*
>   *burnt clean by fire.*

I take off my shoes and in socks
                                        on the Severn's edge
float a clay pot and *paan* leaves.

                          I plop balls of flour -
there are so many they begin to gather around my feet;
landlocked by flowers, rice, cotton threads and god knows what.
Worried that all this will not move
                                (I am aware of people staring),
I almost topple into the river as I aim
throws as far as my stiff neck allows.

I hold you squat in my hands,
open the cap and spill you out.

Solemnly at first, then with a final gush
I swill you out with the water;
muttering a request for peace *Om Shantih Shantih Shantih!*
as you go with the river
                          pulled down into the sea.

Notes:

Shri Ram jaya Ram: a popular mantra in praise of Rama

paan: betel leaf

Om: the primeval sound

Shantih: peace

ELDEST SON

My second child, but my eldest son,
My reason against despair,
                           A wedge
In the door, letting in light.

When you left, without explaining,
I knew you would, like a son, return.

I prayed each day and cried
Your brothers and sisters to sleep.

More precious to me than my own life,
How can you now choose to live apart?

Living in this kitchen, hearing only voices,
Hurts more than your father's blows.

Your leaving, without warning,
Banged shut my life.

SATYENDRA SRIVASTAVA

AT AN ASIAN GIRL'S THIRD WEDDING

Under the jasmine garlanded tent
And rose watered air humidifier
They were there to see Kirpal's daughter
Honourably married

In the reception
They talked
And drank
Talked about Somalias
Bosnias and Sudans
Described the dried up skeletons
The rapes of women
And the situation back home
Ayodhya and its cavity-ridden stone pieces
They talked miles and oceans

They talked and the girl
In the next room was
Weighed down by the golden gifts
Honourably

It was the girl's third wedding
The first in the temple
The second in a London registry office
The third here in the vast reception room
The newsagent Kirpal's accountant watched
Noting down the expenses
On mortgage and bank loan

By midnight they had all left
Leaving behind heaps of food and drinks
And all those talks
Hunger in Somalia
And Bosnia and India
And Pakistan and Bangladesh

Once they left
Worn out women began
Clearing up the leftovers
And
A third world nostalgia.

BETWEEN THOUGHTS

Beyond the missing bits
Between thoughts
The mighty void
The indicator of pain
Completes the blue circle
The mission bell rings
And from the womb of silence
Emerges the nude of desire
Once more I begin to tell the story
With the same old question
How come it's the male peacock
That does all the work
The dancing
The display
The shakes
The hops and the prancing
And at this juncture as usual
A snake rears up
Out of the basket of darkness
Says aloud
Here lies the idea
Suck it, digest it
And vomit it out
Between thoughts
The god of creation
Is bound to emerge.

SIR WINSTON CHURCHILL KNEW MY MOTHER

Sir Winston Churchill he knew India
He knew...
Because India was to him the Kohinoor
Of that Empire on which the sun never sets
Sir Winston also knew the town
Which his people had built for their comfort and ease
Cutting and carving it from the Himalaya's lap
- That child of the icy summits - that town
Which is called Mussoorie
Sir Winston knew where that town was and why
Because he had walked its long street rising and falling
Which had reminded him - somewhere somehow -
Of Princes Street in Edinburgh another
Extremely beautiful town in the British Empire
And Sir Winston knew this too that
Also in the town called Mussoorie
A wave had risen
Shaking the foundations of Britain's Empire
The kind of wave that would seem to him
Just the folly of that crazy naked fakir of
India's national struggle
And Sir Winston knew this too that
In India some women who
Worshipped that same naked fakir as a father
Had lain down one day in the town of Mussoorie
In rows in the road and prevented the units
Of soldiers of the British Empire from going further
And among them had been some women who
Heavy with child could have given birth at any moment...

Therefore... exactly for this reason I
Went to Hyde Park Gate as soon as
I reached London
Stood in front of Sir Winston's shut house
Bowed respectfully, then spoke out loudly -

"You, Sir Winston, know my mother
Pregnant in her eighth month
Having received my father's blessing
She too had lain down in
That road in Mussoorie
From where the army units had to return -
I am the son born from that mother's womb
And Satyendra is my name
And I have come to tell you
That I have now arrived in England..."

SHRIPATI UPADHYAYA

KISS IN THE MEADOWS

Walking in the
meadows
and
stopping to catch a breath,
I saw this:
sun rays
filtering through the leaves.

They stayed
on your face.
In a sudden glimpse
there was this glow of red
on your face.

And to give you
shade,
I planted
a kiss.

THE LONDON AUTUMN

It was damp and cold,
people had bleak faces,
young and old.

Trees were bare with rusty leaves,
some becoming dry,
some saying goodbye.

I was dreading the winter.
I collected myself
as I passed by a lass
selling roses at Piccadilly Circus.
"Roses, red roses, Sir,
for your beloved."

And the next moment
I was buying flowers -
but you were not here yet.

I walked along with a smile.
I was chasing a summer dream.

MAHENDRA K VERMA

it's me

the telephone rang.
i like talking on the telephone
only if someone else rings.
i leap into the dark corridor.
i know how to prolong the conversation.
i chat for half an hour
at their cost
of course.

i like talking on the phone.
i feel at ease, can say anything
that i can't when i face them.

i promise a friend
i'll ring him or her at 8.
i know i'm not going to.
she waits and he waits,
they all wait.
they think
i must have forgotten
and so they ring.
i jump off my bed or settee
with a smile
which they can't see or hear,
and say, "O HELLO! i'm so sorry
.... do ring again."

THE PAST

The past is what I treasure,
the present is what I am
trying to explore
and understand.

The past is what I treasure,
the present is fluid.
The future is written in invisible ink
but the past is heritage
written in indelible ink.

The past can be reborn
and relived.
You know why?
Because the past is what I know.
The present is unstable
and the future unknown.
Is there anything
independent of the past
that you know?

KANTA WALKER

LORD OF MY BURNING PASSIONS

Lord of my burning passions,
pinnacle of my desire,

I have thrown conformity
out of the window.
It lies all tangled,
shrivelled up, dying
in a prickly bush.

Now we sing and dance all night
in illuminated
dance halls of desire,
twin souls in rapturous passion.
A thousand mirrors
cast your reflection,
magnifying your frame
from every angle.
What exquisite beauty and charm
you possess, my Lord!

I have given up
looking for approval
in respectable corners
I am forbidden
to enter.
Condemned by
family and friends,
I dance in defiance.
I don't care
for respectability,
run rings around ridicule.
What does it matter
if I am called a crazy woman!

Dressed in petunia silk,
I dance in defiance
before my love,
in the chamber of my heart.
I am a young bride,

married to my celestial lover.
My heart's ruler,
my heaven on earth,
is doing two steps with me.

Drums are beating now,
the rhythm and tempo
are getting ever faster.
I curl, I twirl,
I swirl, I whirl,
I take off and float.
Tenderly held
in your strong arms,
I have no fear of falling.

You, my peacock lover,
bewitch me with your charms.

KEEPING WATCH

Narrow strip of land
covered with long grass
and uneven footfalls -
I have measured Autumn,
kept a lookout for Spring
and counted dandelions.

I waited in earnestness
for the Summer,
controlling calmly
all passion, all desire.
I danced with the
leafy green trees
and helped magpies
build their nests.
I saw the river change and grow
with each footfall.

It is Autumn now.
In the yellowing trees
and long seeded grass,
in the tangle of rosehips
and prickly blackberries,
in the sweet purples
of the Himalayan Balsam,
I seem to have lost
my endurance and patience,
as if running has
no purpose to it anymore!

GOPI WARRIER

CRICKET AT LORDS

Living behind Lords
I don't have to be
at the grounds or watch T.V.
to know the score.

Each time there is grand
applause England has scored a four.
Polite applause is the opposition's
six. A deafening roar that shakes
the house is an Aussie wicket
or the L.B.W. of Tendulkar.
Pin-drop silence means England
wickets are falling like ninepins.

Last summer, by the lake in Regents Park
birds singing, world bright
and cheery I pass
a short, balding man in a fading three piece,
barrister's brief case underarm.
Perhaps an old Harrovian cricket fan.
He walks slowly, "a schoolboy with his satchel"
and a heavy heart.

On his boyish face is gloom.
The bright day
cannot touch his heart normally languid in the sun.
Obviously England has lost the Match.
Sadly I let him pass knowing his grief
but still long to commiserate
him for a sunny day
when all was perfect
except the score.

R.E.M.

God's sleep is the dream
of our existence. Neurons
of his dream crackle
an explosion of galaxies.
The birth of life is imminent, in
the next rapid eye movement.

In his dark body, as he sleeps
I see a white lotus creeping up
from the right atrium
into the throat.

He should soon awake, glowing
in pure consciousness.

My dream will cease.

EILEEN WRIGHT

THE EARRINGS

Ears
pierced by experience
sites of historical erosion
hearing word-slurs subtle meanings hints
provoked by gifts from abroad
like all those clothes i never wore
through lack of pride or too much shame
who knows i didn't know who i was going to wear
those tenuously thin bright embroidered
bits of culture for

Soon it came too easy too easy not to
celebrate my difference
the one i'd always stored inside
in case i overheard their dirty words
in case in case friends thought me strange
in case their friendship turned to hate
simply for what i wore

Hidden in mothers' English jewel case
dancing girls' earrings lie
sight of them stored
small curled beings ornate and white
makes my time retrace:
Eleven and in love
i needed them so much
pale beaded tassels
their sheer length seduced me
left me longing for their touch
round my mostly European face
but mother never listened never let me
however hard i tried and craved
now she's gone unplanned
they're here - at last
inside my aging hand
the Earrings
unseen
unworn
always saved
living on.

THEY WERE READY

They were ready for the journey Home
talk would come around to this
'the place we left behind'
but Home was invention, glorified dream
no one was waiting there
They were ready
for their second migration
Out of India this time
first they'd left Ireland
hoping for new lives
leaving everything behind
And they were ready
but 1947 was a shock
dream became uneasy reality
suddenly saying goodbye
to several hundred years
though they were seen
by everyone as interlopers now
perhaps they'd always been
They were ready
but two centuries
of travelling wearies the soul
all they knew was how to take risks
to move into a new place
as if they owned it.

VOICES

i am a child in time
who's lost the voices of the past
familiar sounds i took for granted
thought would last
anti-European rise and fall
of my grandmother
as she gossiped
over endless cups of hot sweet tea
rising rising rising
and falling
over me
and the people
she brought with her
with names like Smiler
Duchess and Slim
the man who always wore
dark glasses
never spoke to me
looking from
his one brown one blue eye
East and West met
in him uneasily
while i sat listening
child in the corner
while they flowed on
voices echoing in each other
rising rising rising
and falling
over me.

ABOUT THE CONTRIBUTORS

Daisy Abey was born in Matara, Sri Lanka, and studied at the University of Ceylon. She migrated to Britain in 1965 and is now settled in Leeds. She has written a novel in her native Sinhalese, *Gimhana Ahase Tharaka* ('The Stars in the Summer Sky') which she is translating into English. Under Barry Tebb's guidance, she has been writing poetry seriously for some years. In 1999 she had two booklets of poems in English published by the Sixties Press: *Letter to a Friend: First Poems* and *City of Leeds*.

Shanta Acharya was born in Cuttack in Orissa, India. After completing her MA in English Literature from Ravenshaw College, Cuttack, she went to Oxford in 1979. There she wrote her doctoral thesis on *Emerson and India*. In 1983-84 she was a Visiting Scholar at Harvard. She lives in London where she has worked as an Investment Manager in the City. Her poetry collections include *Not This, Not That* (Rupa, 1994) and *Numbering Our Days' Illusions* (Rockingham Press, 1995).

Shafi Ahmed was born in Bangladesh in 1937 and came to the UK in 1952 to study marine engineering. He has travelled the world as an engineer in the Merchant Navy. He retired from Civil Service in 1996 and appeared on television's 'Mastermind' programme the following year. The author of several scientific and mathematical books, he is also a bilingual poet and literary translator. Shafi Ahmed's translations of Rabindranath Tagore's selected poems are published as *Tagore's Eleven* (1985). His poem, 'Bedeh', won a Peterloo Poets Prize in 1992.

Shenaz Ali is studying BA (Hon.) English Studies at Huddersfield University. She writes poetry and fiction. She is being published for the first time and admits to feeling "slightly shocked".

Moniza Alvi was born in Pakistan in 1954 and grew up in Hertfordshire. Her first poetry collection, *The Country at My Shoulder* (OUP, 1993), was shortlisted for the T S Eliot and the Whitbread poetry prizes, and was selected for The Poetry Society's New Generation Poets promotion. *A Bowl of Warm Air* (OUP, 1996) was included in *The Independent on Sunday* 'Books of the Year'. Bloodaxe will publish her new collection, *Carrying My Wife*, in 2000. After a long career as a secondary school teacher, Moniza now lives in South West London with her husband and daughter, Alice, born 1997. She works part-time as a freelance writer and a tutor for the Open College of the Arts.

Shamim Azad was born in Mymensingh, East Pakistan (present-day Bangladesh). At 14 she went as a Girl Guide to a summer camp in Muree where she kept a detailed diary, published in the Bengali newspaper, *Dainik Azad*. She now lives in London where she works as a teacher, freelance journalist and playwright. She has published three poetry collections, a volume of short stories, two novels and a collection of her articles - all in Bengali. She has also edited a bi-lingual anthology, *Voyages*. For details of her books and activities visit her website at http://www.theazads.freeserve.co.uk/shamim.htm

Mariya Aziz is a student in Leeds. Interested in writing, she participated during summer 1998 in the Adab Creative Writing Project in Leeds.

Dileep Bagnall says that he "is and intends to be for some time. Was educated. Lives somewhere. Is annoyingly secretive and glad to be mad."

Rajat Kumar Biswas was born in India and graduated from the University of Calcutta's Presidency College. After working in various public libraries in London, he spends his retirement in Ilford and takes a keen interest in travel, swimming, cricket and photography. A bi-lingual poet, his publications include: *A Flat for Sale and Other Poems* (1987), *Mukhosh O Anyanya Kabita* (1993) and *The Lascar's Song* (1995).

Sindamani Bridglal was born in Guyana, but migrated to Britain with her family when she was nine years old. She is now based in London where she works as a script writer and film-maker.

Varun Chandra was born in North Shields in 1984. He is a student at the Royal Grammar School, Newcastle. From an early age he has been fascinated by English Literature and has been encouraged by his parents and teachers to experiment with language. Much of his time is occupied with dance, music, martial arts, languages and sports.

Debjani Chatterjee was born in Delhi in 1952 and came to Britain in 1972 via Japan, Bangladesh, Hong Kong, Egypt and Morocco. She studied at universities in Cairo, Canterbury, Lancaster and Sheffield. She has worked in the steel industry, education and community relations. Her poetry books are: *I Was That Woman* (Hippopotamus), *The Sun Rises in the North* (Smith/Doorstop), *A Little Bridge* (Pennine Pens) and *Albino Gecko* (University of Salzburg). Widely anthologised, her poems have won various prizes including a Peterloo Poets prize. She won a Yorkshire & Humberside Arts Writer's Award in 1995. She has translated books and co-edited some bi-lingual ones, including *Barbed Lines* which won the Raymond Williams Community Publishing Prize. Her books for children include *The Elephant-Headed God & Other Hindu Tales*, selected for Children's Books of the Year 1990. She is Reviews Editor of *Writing in Education*, published by the National Association of Writers in Education. For a list of her books visit NAWE's website at http://www.nawe.co.uk

Samir Chatterjee grew up in an Indian steel town and wrote Bengali poetry as a teenager. He was a student editor of the Scottish Church College Literary Magazine in Calcutta. After studying at the London School of Economics he was a successful community development worker in the 1970's. He joined the Liverpool Writers' Club and began writing poetry in English. Later he was Senior Community Education Officer in Rochdale, but retired early and trained as an adult education teacher. In 1997 he won a scholarship to pursue PhD research at Manchester University. He has written widely on environmental education, housing and community work. Poems have appeared in various anthologies.

Mary Dammyenty Chauhan was born in 1965. She is a bi-lingual Gujerati poet and playwright, based in Derby. She won an East Midlands Arts Writer's Bursary in 1990 and her play, 'Red Skies', came second in the 'Kalam Kahe' AsianPlaywriting Competition run by the BBC Pebble Mill, Leicester Haymarket Theatre and SAMPAD. She has also received two Prince's Trust Awards. Her work has been performed at various prestigious venues and broadcast on radio, including Radio 4's 'South Asian Poetry and Songs'. It has been anthologised in *Mothercountry Fatherland* (Tak Tak Tak), *You'll Love This Stuff* (Cambridge University Press) and *Allegator Raggedy-Mouth* (A & C Black), and published in magazines like *Kunapipi*, *Staple* and *The National Anti-Racist Movement in Education*.

Maya Chowdhry is a Sheffield-based inTer-aCt-ive artist, award winning playwright and poet, and has been working professionally since 1989. She has five plays for BBC radio and five for the stage (small-scale touring and Regional Rep) to her credit. From 1987-1994 she worked as a filmmaker, photographer and Live Artist creating multimedia works. Her poetry has been published widely - most recently in *Healing Strategies for Women at War: Seven Black Women Poets* (Crocus Books). She is currently working on a CD-*ROM* poetic piece - *Destiny* - which uses moving and still image, spoken and written text to take the audience on a journey from *kala pani* to *gorah zamin* ('black waters to white lands').

Saleha Chowdhury was born in Rajshahi, Bangladesh in 1943 and came to Britain in 1972. She has written several books of fiction and poetry in Bengali and one collection of poems in English, *Broad Canvas* (1997). She is a primary school teacher in Tower Hamlets, London, and has two grown-up children. She explains her compulsion for writing poetry: 'I have bottled-up emotions and when the genie in the bottle screams, I sit at the desk with pad and pen.'

David Dabydeen was born and raised on a sugar plantation in Guyana. He read English at Cambridge and London Universities, completing his doctorate in 1982. He is presently Professor of Caribbean Studies at the University of Warwick. His first poetry collection, *Slave Song*, won the Commonwealth Poetry Prize in 1984. This was followed by *Coolie Odyssey* (1988), and *Turner* (1994). His novels include *The Intended* (1991), *Disappearance* (1993), *The Counting House* (1996) and *A Harlot's Progress* (1999). He has been hailed as 'the best of the younger generation of Caribbean novelists, writing powerfully about the immigrant experience'.

Ketaki Kushari Dyson was born in Calcutta in 1940 and educated at Calcutta and Oxford. She has been based in England since her marriage to an Englishman. An award-winning author, she has published five collections of Bengali poetry, with another forthcoming, and novels, plays and literary criticism. Her first play was premiered in Manchester City of Drama 1994. A distinguished translator, her *Selected Poems* of Rabindranath Tagore (Bloodaxe, 1991) was a Poetry Book Society Recommended Translation. She is currently translating Buddhadeva Bose's poetry. Her research-based books include a study of the journals and memoirs of the British in India in 1765-1856; the relationship between Tagore and Victoria Ocampo; and a study of the effects of protanopia on Tagore's work. Poetry collections in English include: *Sap-Wood* (Writers Workshop, 1978), *Hibiscus in the North* (pamphlet, Mid-Day Publications, 1979), *Spaces I Inhabit* (Navana, 1983), and *Memories of Argentina and Other Poems* (Virgilio Libro, 1999). For a list of her books visit her website at http://www.ketaki.dyson.dial.pipex.com

Jeanne Ellin is a poet and storyteller who lives in Yorkshire. She comes from an Anglo-Indian family.

Yasmin Farooq was born and brought up in Azad Kashmir and came to England in 1977. She is married and has two children, Zana and Faroz. Since 1981 she has been working for Social Services in Sheffield. She enjoys attending mushairas and reading books by other South Asian women. Her poems have appeared in magazines and anthologies.

Saqi Farooqi is the pen name of Qazi Muhammad Shamshad Nabi Farooqi. He was born in Gorakhpur, North India, in 1936. In 1947 his family migrated to Bangladesh, then in 1950 to Karachi in Pakistan. Saqi Farooqi came to England to study English Literature, married an Austrian, became an accountant/programmer and settled in London. Sometimes regarded as an *enfant terrible* of Urdu Literature, he is also one of the leading Urdu poets of his generation. He has been attending workshops run by the Highgate Poets and occasionally writes poems in English. His Urdu books include: *Pyaas kaa sahraa*, *Raazo se bharaa bastah* and *Bahraam kii vaapasii*. Readers in English can access his work in *A Listening Game* (Lokamaya Press), *Haji Bhai Pani-Wala* (Highgate Poets) and *Nailing Dark Storms* (Hub Editions).

Romesh Gunasekera was born in Sri Lanka and came to Britain in 1972. His poems have received several awards, and have been published in various literary magazines and newspapers. His first novel, *Reef*, was shortlisted for the 1994 Booker Prize and won one of the five continents Premio Mondello awards in Italy. His most recent novel, *The Sandglass*, received the new BBC Asia Award for Writing in 1998.

Prabhu Siddhartha Guptara was born in New Delhi in 1949. He writes, lectures and broadcasts widely. He has two collections of poems ("grandiloquently titled *Beginnings* and *Continuations*"), he edited *The Collected Poems of Leela Dharmaraj*, and put together the first annotated bibliography of *Black British Literature* from the eighteenth century to the present.

Zorina Ishmail-Bibby was born in Guyana and migrated to Britain in the 1960's. She lives in Northampton where she was County Co-ordinator for ESOL, and later lecturer at Northampton College. She was also Chair of NATECLA in 1989/90. A keen environmentalist, she chairs the St. George's Community and Wildlife Group. She also paints and facilitates the Chameleon Writers' Cooperative. A poetry collection, *After a Cold Season - Rising*, was published in 1988. Zorina's short stories and poems have won various prizes and been published in magazines and anthologies, and broadcast on radio. In 1994 she was awarded an East Midlands Arts Bursary to complete her novel, *The Outcasts: Corentyne Scandal*.

Mahmood Jamal was born in Lucknow, India in 1948 and came to Britain from Pakistan in 1967. He graduated in South Asian Studies from the School of Oriental and African Studies, University of London. He is a poet, translator, film producer, director and founder-member of Retake Film and Video Collective. In 1984 he won the Minority Rights Group Award for poetry and translation and his first poetry collection, *Silence Inside a Gun's Mouth*, was published. He is also the compiler and translator of *The Penguin Book of Modern Urdu Poetry* (1986).

Shahidah Janjua lives in Sheffield. Jointly with Maya Chowdhry and Seni Seneviratne, she has published a poetry anthology, *Putting in the Pickle Where the Jam Should Be* (Jag Rahi Hai and Write Back, Sheffield Libraries, 1989).

Mohammad Hafeez Johar was born in Rawalpindi, Pakistan in 1954 and came to Britain in 1968. He studied at Bradford College, graduating in Organisation Studies, then did a Postgraduate Diploma in Librarianship. He works for Bradford Library Services. His first poetry collection in Urdu, *Barf Ka Rog* ('The Curse of Snow') was published in Pakistan in 1995.

Parm Kaur - Parm Kaur hails from a Punjabi Indian background and is a London-based performance poet who has appeared at prestigious national and international venues. She is also an experienced workshop leader. She has appeared on Channel 4's 'Big Breakfast' programme and her poems have been broadcast on various radio programmes. Her work has been anthologised in *The Fire People* (Payback Press) and *Bittersweet* (Women's Press). She was the Thames Valley FM Writer in Residence in 1997 and received the Saccan Award from Southern Arts in 1998.

Shamshad Khan was born in Leeds in 1964 and now lives in Manchester where she has worked for the Low Pay Unit and Manchester City Council. She is a poet and short story writer whose work is published in various anthologies, including *Bittersweet* (The Women's Press), T*he Fire People* (Payback Press) and *Healing Strategies for Women at War* (Crocus).

Sitara Khan was born in Karachi in Pakistan, but came to England at 14. Her mother tongue is Punjabi and she sometimes sings in Urdu. The author of *A Glimpse Through Purdah* (Trentham Books, 1999), she works as an Education Officer in Leeds and also writes short stories and plays. She is currently writing a novel.

Usha Kishore is from Kerala in South India and now lives in Kent where she is a teacher.

Khan Singh Kumar teaches in a London secondary school. He writes "mainly dramatic monologues with a strong post-colonial awareness". His poems have won prizes and been commended in various competitions, and have been published in many literary magazines, including *Staple, The Rialto, Krax, Poetry London Newsletter* and *Poetry Ireland Review.*

Tariq Latif was born in a village near Lahore, Pakistan, in 1962. He spent his early childhood on his grandfather's farm. His family moved to Manchester in 1970. He studied Physics at the University of Sheffield and has worked in a Cash and Carry shop, fashion shops and as a part-time roadie. His poetry collections are *Skimming the Soul* and *The Minister's Garden.*

Asit Maitra was born in Jalpaiguri in West Bengal. From an early age he had a tutor at home who encouraged him in his love of literature, both Bengali and English. After training as a surgeon in Calcutta, he came to Britain and has worked for the National Health Service since 1962. He lives in Newcastle where he is a Consultant Surgeon at the Royal Victoria Infirmary. He has had a poetry pamphlet, *Zig-Zags*, published jointly with Pat Borthwick in 1998.

Soumyen Maitra was born in India and now lives in Merseyside. He works as a doctor in Manchester. His poetry and short stories in Bengali and English have appeared in magazines and anthologies. He also edits and publishes a bi-lingual magazine, *Naba Diganta /New Horizon.*

Srabanti Maitra has been living in the UK since the age of seven. After attending private schools, she graduated in English Literature and is now a final year Law student.

Roohi Majid was born in India where she studied Urdu and English Literature. She obtained a doctorate in Urdu and taught at Bihar University before coming to England in the 1970's. Settled in London, she takes an active interest in community relations. After voluntary retirement from a deputy headship in 1997, Roohi engages full-time in bi-lingual writing (mainly poetry), translating, painting and other creative pursuits. She is a member of the Camden Poetry Group and co-ordinates the Multi-lingual Poetry Forum.

Anjum Malik was born in Dharan, Saudi Arabia, then returned with her family to Pakistan when she was seven. She attended school in Rawalpindi for four years before her family migrated to England. She now lives in Manchester but travels extensively. Her various jobs have included being a Police Officer, an interpreter, an Outreach Worker for the Asian Women Writers' Collective and Literature Development Officer for the Black Literature Project. She was writer-in-residence for the Asian community in Blackburn in 1991 and for HTV in Bristol in 1998/99. She has an MA in Scriptwriting for Film and Television and has various screen plays and TV scripts to her credit. Her poetry collection, *Before the Rains* (Huddersfield University Press, 1996), is soon to be followed by a second, *Love Games*.

Samia Malik is based in Norwich and is a writer, composer and singer whose work is rooted in the traditional ghazal. She is part of a performance group called Garam Masala who have produced a CD entitled *The Colour of the Heart* (Sound & Language, 1998).

Divya Mathur has three poetry collections in Hindi. She also writes short fiction in Hindi and has edited an anthology of short stories. She is Senior Administrator at the Nehru Centre in London.

Irfan Merchant is 25 and lives and studies in Edinburgh. His father is Indian and mother English, while Irfan describes himself as Scottish-Asian.

Naeem Mirza lives in Halifax.

Shabnam Mujaver is of Indian origin and lives in Liversedge.

Trilokesh Mukherjee was born in Gauhati, India in 1938. He is a graphic designer and has taught this subject for many years. He was awarded a Radhakrishnan Fellowship at the University of Oxford in 1981. His interests include: jazz, blues, folk songs, and water colours. He also writes poetry in Bengali.

Raman Mundair is a poet, playwright, scriptwriter, singer, actress and educationalist. Born in Ludhiana, India, she now lives in London. She frequently performs her own work and facilitates creative workshops. Her poems have appeared in several anthologies including *The Fire People* (Payback Press) and *Bittersweet* (The Women's Press). Currently writing for Tamasha and Clean Break theatre companies, she is also working on a poetry collection and novel. In 2000 she will be Writer-in-Residence in the Isle of Wight.

Maya Naidoo was born in 1975 to South African parents living in exile in England. Educated at Bournemouth School for Girls and St Hugh's College, Oxford, where she read History, she began training to be a lawyer with a Diplock Scholarship from Middle Temple. She has now taken up a scholarship for a Masters in European Law at the College of Europe in Bruges before completing her professional training for the Bar. She has a strong personal interest in issues of civil liberties and human rights and has travelled widely, exploring some of the many international links in her family. She has made contact with members of her paternal grandfather's family who remained in India when her great-grandfather left as an indentured labourer for Natal, South Africa. In 1995, the year that all South African schools were required to operate a non-racial policy, she taught English to Zulu-speaking children in a formerly all-Indian school and published her first article, 'Changing Education at Parlock Primary'.

Suniti Namjoshi, born in Bombay in 1941, is a poet, critic, satirist and fabulist. She has worked as an Officer in the Indian Administrative Service and held academic posts in India and Canada, before settling in Devon. Her fiction books include: *Feminist Fables*, *The Conversations of Cow*, *The Blue Donkey Fables*, and *Aditi and the one-eyed monkey*, written for children. She has co-translated *Poems of Govindagraj* from Marathi with Sarojini Namjoshi. She is also the author of several volumes of poetry including *The Authentic Lie* and *From the Bedside Book of Nightmares*.

Nazrul Islam Naz was born in Sylhet, Bangladesh, in 1959 and came to Britain in 1973. He lives in London and writes poetry in English and in Bengali.

Michael Nazir-Ali was born in 1949 and graduated from Karachi University in 1970. After an MLitt from both Cambridge and Oxford, he did a PhD at the University of New South Wales. Currently Bishop of Rochester and Visiting Professor in Theology and Religious Studies at Greenwich University, his recent books include *The Mystery of Faith* and *Citizens and Exiles: Christian Faith in a Plural World*.

Naranjan Singh Noor was born in the Punjab in 1933 and was a teacher before moving to Britain in 1965. Married with four children, he has been a labourer, postman, teacher, Race Equality Adviser and retired in 1997 as Director of Community Education at Bilston Community College, Wolverhampton. He was active in the Indian Workers Association and, as General Secretary of the Progressive Writers' Association, he took a lead in setting up an MA Punjabi course at Bilston Community College. He has published six poetry collections in Punjabi, one in English: *The Best Friday*, and also edited a bi-lingual poetry anthology. His Punjabi poetry has won a number of awards.

Hugo Saleel Nurbhai writes poetry, fiction, articles and literary criticism. He has taught in adult and higher education, and is currently working part-time as a research assistant in the Department of Languages and International Studies at the University of Central Lancashire. He also runs workshops as part of the Lancaster Literature Festival creative writing team. He won a George Eliot Fellowship in 1994.

Kauser Parveen lives in Halifax.

Yogesh Patel was born in Kenya, migrated to Uganda, and then went to India where he studied optometry and became active in the literary scene. He now lives in Surrey. A bi-lingual writer in Gujarati and English, he is also co-editor of *Skylark* - an international quarterly on contemporary literature in translation, and is a past President of the Gujarati Literary Academy. His books in English are a poetry collection, *The Manikin in Exile*, and a children's picture book, *Magic Glasses*. In Gujarati he has a poetry collection, *Ahin*, and a collection of short stories, *Pagalani Lipi*. Yogesh Patel also has four L.P. records (in Hindi and Gujarati) and an English film (*The Last Days of Gandhi*) to his credit. Among numerous awards, he has received the 'freedom of the city of London'.

Kailash G Puri was born in Rawalpindi in British India and studied at the Women's College, Lahore. After an arranged marriage to an Indian scientist, Dr Gopal S Puri, she accompanied him to Nigeria, Ghana and then England. She taught yoga and Indian cookery for many years, and also edited *Subhagwali* and *Roopvati* magazines in Punjabi. But she is best known as Britain's first Asian agony aunt and has worked extensively in this capacity for Punjabi magazines and newspapers, and appeared on numerous radio and television programmes. She has written over thirty books in Punjabi: novels, short stories, essays, poetry, books on cookery and sexology, and her acclaimed autobiography, *Bari Jaon Lakh Beria*. From the 1980's onwards she has won several important Punjabi literary awards.

Padmaja Rao was born in India and studied English Literature at Patna

University. She now lives in Sunderland with her family and two rabbits. Her interests include painting, Indo-Anglian Literature and writing poems and short stories in English and Hindi. She has co-edited a multilingual poetry anthology, *Poetry in Action* (Kala Sangam, 1999).

Ian Iqbal Rashid was born in Dar-es-Salaam in 1965, grew up in Toronto and moved to England in 1990. He now lives in Bristol. His poetry collections are: *Black Markets, White Boyfriends and Other Acts of Elision* (Tsar Press, Toronto, 1991), nominated for Canada's Gerald Lampert Prize; *Song of Sabu* (disOrientation Chapbooks, Calgary, 1994); and *The Heat Yesterday* (Coach House Press, Toronto, 1995). He has written widely for British radio and television, including the multi-award winning TV series, *This Life*, for which he and his co-writers won the prestigious Writer's Guild of England award for best writing for a TV series. In 1998 he wrote and directed his first short film, 'Surviving Sabu', which won Special Jury Prizes at Vancouver's Out on Screen festival and at the Festival of Dhow Countries in Zanzibar. He received the 1998 Aga Khan Award of Excellence for the Arts.

Selina Rodrigues is of Indian-English parentage and is often assumed to be Iranian, Irish or Spanish. She lives in London. She has not had anything published previously.

Saiqah Salim was born in Bradford in 1978. She began to write seriously only after the breakdown of her marriage. She writes in both Urdu and English. Other interests include reading, music, sports and spending time with her son, Haroon. She would like all barriers between people to be broken and believes that poetry has the power to achieve this.

Ashoka Sen lives in Chesterfield where she is a member of the Chesterfield Writers' Club. She has an MA in Creative Writing from Sheffield Hallam University and wrote her first novel, *The Daughter of Mountains*, under the supervision of Jane Rogers. She also writes short stories and poems, some of which have been published and broadcast on radio.

Sati Sen was educated in India and worked as a Language Support Team teacher in Tower Hamlets, London. She is very interested in South Asian Literature. After retirement she attended creative writing classes and has had a few poems published.

Sudeep Sen was born in 1964 in New Delhi. He studied Literature there and in the USA. As an Inlaks Scholar he completed an MS in Journalism from Columbia University, New York. His poetry collections include: *The Lunar Visitations* (1990), *New York Times* (1993), *Dali's Twisted Hands* (1995) and *Postmarked India: New & Selected Poems* (1997). A recipient of numerous awards, Sen also works as a literary columnist and editor.

Seni Seneviratne was born in Yorkshire in 1951 to an English mother and Sri Lankan father. She lives in Sheffield where she has worked in post-16 education since 1975. She is a founder member of the Awaaz educational project for Asian women. Apart from being a poet and performer, she is also a writer, singer and photographer. She has a poetry and song collection on audio tape, *Climbing Mountains*, and has contributed to many anthologies including *Charting the Journey: Writings by Black and Third World Women* (Sheba), *Putting in the Pickle where the Jam should be* (Jag Rahi Hai) and *Healing Strategies for Women at War* (Crocus Books). She was a runner up in the Poetry Business 'Black Writers Week' and was joint second with her poem, 'Cinnamon', in the Margot Jane Memorial Prize in association with Only women Press. For a list of her books visit NAWE's website at http://www.nawe.co.uk

Khadija Shahjahan was born in 1955 in Bangladesh. She now lives in London, but while living in Doncaster she joined the BWSG Book Project who published her travel book, (*Europey Banglar Meye*, 1995), a collection of essays (*E Juger Kotha Mala*, 1999) and two poetry collections (*Protichhobi*, 1995, and *Anubhobey Ami*, 1999), all in Bengali. She is also a freelance journalist contributing to Bengali newspapers and serves as a Governor of Doncaster Deaf College. Married to a doctor, she has two grown-up children.

Taslima Shahjahan was born in 1973 in Dhaka, Bangladesh, and brought up in England. A Business Studies graduate from the University of Sheffield, she is currently working as a Human Resources Consultant in a national company. She enjoys writing poetry in both Bengali and English as a hobby, and many of her poems have been published in magazines and anthologies. She hopes to have a collection published soon.

John Siddique was born in 1964. He is a Manchester-based freelance multi media artist who works with writing, performance, electronic sound, sampling, music, film, graphics, visual and live art. He often runs workshops in schools, colleges and prisons, and also runs Jowonio Productions, specialising in innovative spoken word based recordings. His publications include *the devil's lunchbox* (Mongrel Press, 1998) and a few albums. His poetry has appeared in many anthologies and magazines, and been broadcast on radio and television.

Durlabh Singh was born in Nairobi, Kenya and came to Britain at the age of twenty. He is a self-taught artist who works in oils, watercolours and pen and ink. His work has been exhibited in India, Kenya and all over Britain. He is a founder member of Rainbow Art Group - a group of artists from 'third world' countries, and of the National Artists Association of Great Britain, as well as being active in several other visual artists' and writers' groups. His art reviews, articles and poems have been published widely.

Gerry Singh was born in Glasgow in 1957, of an Indian father and Scottish mother, and brought up by foster parents. After leaving school without formal qualifications, he returned to study as a mature student with the Open University. He obtained an MA Honours in English Literature and now teaches in a secondary school. His great love for the Scottish Highlands is reflected in his poetry.

Mahendra Solanki was born in 1956 in Nairobi and now lives in Leicester. His poetry collections include *Shadows of my Making* (Lokamaya Press, 1986), *What You Leave Behind* (Blackwater Press, 1996), *Exercises in Trust* (Aark Arts, 1996) and a selection of new poems in *The Rat's Mirror* (Ha'penny Press, 1999). Mahendra is Course Leader of the MA in Writing programme at The Nottingham Trent University and an editor for Blackwater Press.

Satyendra Srivastava was born in India, but has lived in the UK for nearly four decades. He lectures at the Faculty of Oriental Studies, University of Cambridge. A well-known Hindi writer, he has published many collections of Hindi poetry, plays and radio plays, and has been a columnist for various Indian publications. He also broadcasts in both Hindi and English, and is a corresponding editor of *Ambit*. His poetry collections in English are *Talking Sanskrit to Fallen Leaves* (Peepal Tree Press, 1995) and *Between Thoughts* (Samvad Prakashan, 1998).

Shripati Upadhyaya was born in 1947 at Varanasi, India, and came to the UK in 1990. He is a Consultant Clinical Psychologist with the Learning Disability Directorate, Bradford Community Health NHS Trust. He is one of the founders of the well known South Asian arts organisation, Kala Sangam. His mother tongue is Hindi and he is a bi-lingual poet and translator. He has co-edited the multi-lingual poetry anthologies, *The*

Northern Durbar (1997), and *Poems of Cultural Diversity* (1999). He lives in Sherburn-in-Elmet near Leeds.

Mahendra K Verma lectured in English Literature in India before coming to Britain where he has been teaching and researching in ESL, Hindi and 'endangered' languages at the University of York for over two decades. He writes poetry in Hindi and English, but is generally reluctant to share them with others. Along with his wife, the Hindi writer, Usha Verma, he is a founder member of the Bhartiya Bhasha Sangam which holds multi-lingual literary events.

Kanta Walker is a poet and novelist in Punjabi and English. She has worked in education and in psychotherapy. Her interests include spending time with her grandchildren, travel, painting and the mystical love poems of Mira Bai.

Gopi Warrier comes from a distinguished family of poets, administrators and physicians in Kerala, India. He graduated in English Literature and did an MBA in International Business at the London Business School, the Ecole des Hautes Commerciales in Paris and the New York University Graduate School of Business. He is the Chairman of a management consulting firm and of an Alternative Medical company in London. He is the author of *The Complete Illustrated Guide to Ayurveda* (Element Books) and three collections of poetry, the latest being *Lament of JC* (The Delhi London Poetry Foundation, 1999).

Eileen Wright lives in Hebden Bridge. Her long poem sequence, *Migration*, published as a pamphlet by Magnetic Press, explores her Anglo-Indian heritage and the long-term effects of mixed identity, colonialisation and migration. She has co-edited *Empty Vessels*, an anthology by Dean Clough Writers. Very interested in the ways that writing and visual image can interact, she is currently working on a poetry collection, *Rune*, in which she collaborates with graphic designer, Andy Campbell.

Copyright Acknowledgements

The editor and publishers thank the following for permission to print or reprint the selections in this book.

Daisy Abey for 'Only', published in *Letter to a Friend: First Poems* and 'Ghost Games', published in *City of Leeds*, both from Sixties Press.

Shanta Acharya for 'The Night of Shiva', published in *Not This, Not That* (Rupa), and 'My Good Luck Home'.

Shafi Ahmed for 'Bulu's Freedom', published in *Focus* (Society of Civil Service Authors) and 'Bedeh'which won a Peterloo Poets Prize in 1992 and was published in *Poetry Matters*.

Shenaz Ali for 'A Broken Heart'.

Moniza Alvi for 'Takeaway','Queen-of-the-Night', published in *Scratch*, and 'Thoughts of a Pakistani Woman in an English Jail', broadcast on the BBC World Service & published in *The Independent*.

Shamim Azad for 'Eclipse of Moonlight' and 'Twofold'.

Mariya Aziz for 'Solitude' and 'Alien Abduction'.

Dileep Bagnall for 'Negotiations', published in *Iota*, 'If You Jump', and 'Not Paranoid But Practical'.

Rajat Kumar Biswas for 'Cambridge' and 'September, 1987', both published in *The Lascar's Song*.

Sindamani Bridglal for 'She Lives Between Back Home and Home', published in *Watchers & Seekers* (The Women's Press).

Varun Chandra for 'Bee'.

Debjani Chatterjee for 'To the English Language', published in *I Was That Woman* (Hippopotamus Press), and 'Visiting E M Forster', and 'Not Your Average Snake', both published in *A Little Bridge* (Pennine Pens). 'To the English Language' was a winning entry in the Peterloo Poets Open Poetry Competition in 1989 and 'Visiting E M Forster' was a winning entry in the Southport Writers' Circle Open Poetry Competition in 1992.

Samir Chatterjee for 'Hillsborough'. An extract was previously published in *Flame* (Crocus Books).

Mary Dammyenty Chauhan for 'Betel Nut', published in *Kunapipi*, and 'My Mother', published in *Poetry Nottingham International*.

Maya Chowdhry for 'Brides of Dust', which won the 1992 Cardiff International Poetry Competition and was published in *Risk Behaviour: the Poetry Business Competition Anthology, 1993*; and 'My Eyes' and 'What is Racism?'

Saleha Chowdhury for 'Existentialism', published in *A Broad Canvas*, and 'A Bottle of Perfume', published in *Elements of Life* (Spotlight Poets).

David Dabydeen for 'Coolie Odyssey', published in *Coolie Odyssey* (Hansib Publishing & Dangaroo Press).

Ketaki Kushari Dyson for 'Jenny Joseph', 'Herb-Thoughts' and 'Gender, Ethnicity,

Community', all published in *Memories of Argentina and Other Poems* (Virgilio Libro).

Jeanne Ellin for 'A Gift for Grandmother' and 'Grandmother', both published in *The Northern Durbar* (Pontefract Press & Kala Sangam).

Yasmin Farooq for 'Is Biology my Destiny?' published in *Flame* (Crocus Books).

Saqi Farooqi for 'The Lie', and 'Heart -transplant', both published in *Nailing Dark Storms* (Hub Editions).

Romesh Gunesekera for 'Wanderlust', published in the Poetry on the Buses celebration for *London - The Living City* in 1998, 'Frontliners', a version of which was a prizewinning entry in the Peterloo Poets Open Poetry Competition and was published in *Poetry Matters*, and 'Turning Point', a version of which was published in *The London Review of Books*.

Prabhu Siddhartha Guptara for 'Global Warming'.

Zorina Ishmail-Bibby for 'Passport' and "Immigrant' Women', published in *After a Cold Season - Rising*, and 'Adolescence: Girl at Jalousie'. 'Passport' won 2nd Prize in Fagin's Book Shop Poetry Competition in 1987.

Mahmood Jamal for 'Migrants' and 'Entry Certificate'.

Shahidah Janjua for 'Strong and Ancient', published in *Putting in the Pickle Where the Jam Should Be* (Jag Rahi Hai & Write Back, Sheffield Libraries).

Mohammad Hafeez Johar for 'Home', published in *Spirit of Bradford: Poems for the City's Centenary* (Redbeck Press).

Parm Kaur for 'The Breaking', and 'Displacement'.

Shamshad Khan for 'Oppressed Coverage'.

Sitara Khan for 'The Fool's Observation', 'The Knight' and 'Mother-Daughter'.

Usha Kishore for 'Teaching Tagore to 10A/S', published in *The Career Teacher*, and 'You and Me'.

Khan Singh Kumar for 'Kabba Bares his Chest at his Son's Parents' Evening', which was a runner up in the Surrey poetry Competition in 1998, and 'Culture Clash' which won 3rd place in the VB Poetry Prize in 1999.

Tariq Latif for 'Letting Go' and 'Uncle Mustka', in *Skimming the Soul*, and 'The *Chucky*', in *The Minister's Garden*, both published by Arc.

Asit Maitra for 'Thakurdah', and 'Fuhlwalla', both published in *Zig-Zag* (Pharos Press).

Soumyen Maitra for 'Chinese Takeaway' and 'Idea for a Poem'.

Srabanti Maitra for 'Constellation'.

Roohi Majid for 'The Wedding' and 'Khurram'.

Anjum Malik for 'All Alright', published in *Before the Rains* (Huddersfield University Press).

Samia Malik for 'Colour of her Heart' in Garam Masala's CD, *the colour of the heart* (Sound & Language).

Divya Mathur for 'Waves and the Bank'.

Irfan Merchant for 'I'm a racist', published in *Forthwrite* (Edinburgh City Libraries), 'Sadhu', and 'Tableau'.

Naeem Mirza for 'Failure haunts me'.

Shabnam Mujaver for 'Alone', published in *A Lasting Calm* (The International Library of Poetry).

Trilokesh Mukherjee for 'I Remember' and 'Yes, Yes, Memories...'.

Raman Mundair for 'An Elegy for Two Boys' and 'Osmosis'.

Maya Naidoo for 'Ama'.

Suniti Namjoshi for 'Among Tigers', published in *The Blue Donkey Fables* (The Women's Press), 'In that particular temple', published in *Flesh and Paper* (Jezebel Tapes and Books), and 'The Dwarfs'.

Nazrul Islam Naz for 'Roaring Silence' and 'Friday, 6th of March, 1998'.

Michael Nazir-Ali for "Haiku' - Holy Week 1995' and 'Trinity Sunday at Kwangju'.

Naranjan Singh Noor for 'Dunkirk', published in *The Best Friday* (Progressive Writers'Association GB).

Hugo Saleel Nurbhai for 'An Affair of the Heart' and 'Conspiracy Theory'.

Kauser Parveen for 'Dangerous Excitement'.

Yogesh Patel for 'Typical Mr Patel's Typical Promotion' and 'The Values'.

Kailash Puri for 'Circle Line' and 'Karma', both published in *Sphere* (Dynamic Publications).

Padmaja Rao for 'The Journey', published in *Poetry in Action* (Kala Sangam), and 'For You'.

Ian Iqbal Rashid for 'Another Country', a version of which was published in *Black Markets, White Boyfriends and Other Acts of Elision* (Tsar Press), and 'Returning to Canada', published in *The Heat Yesterday* (Coach House Press).

Selina Rodrigues for 'Missing' and 'Museum'.

Saiqah Salim for 'You Take Me'.

Ashoka Sen for 'My ending is like my beginning' and 'The Past like the Chorus Character'.

Sati Sen for 'My Dear Friend', published in *A Lasting Calm* (The International Library of Poetry), and 'Stone'.

Sudeep Sen for 'Flying Home', published in *Postmarked India* (HarperCollins India), 'Translating Poetry', published in *Dali's Twisted Hands* (Peepal Tree Press), and 'Dadu', published in *Kali in Ottava Rima* (Paramount).

Seni Seneviratne for 'Just Jealous', published in *Putting in the Pickle where the Jam should be* (Jag Rahi Hai), 'Lena Rulak', published in *Healing Strategies for Women at War* (Crocus Books), and 'Cinnamon Roots' which won 2nd Prize in the Margot Jane Memorial Poetry Prize in association with Only women Press in 1993.

Khadija Shahjahan for 'Tuberose'.

Taslima Shahjahan for 'London'.

John Siddique for 'perfume', in *Kiss*, 'blues for Ambedkar', in *Nailing Colours*, both published by Crocus Books; and 'neckgrip'.

Durlabh Singh for 'Lady of my Dreams'.

Gerry Singh for 'Ladhar Bheinn', 'India Gate' and 'In My Love's Eyes'.

Mahendra Solanki for 'In a Jar' and 'Eldest Son', both published in *What You Leave*

Behind (Blackwater Press), and 'After a while you believe the lies you tell'.

Satyendra Srivastava for 'At an Asian Girl's Third Wedding' and 'Between Thoughts', both published in *Between Thoughts* (Samvad), and 'Sir Winston Churchill Knew My Mother'.

Shripati Upadhyaya for 'Kiss in the Meadows' and 'The London Autumn'

Mahendra K Verma for 'it's me' and 'The Past'.

Kanta Walker for 'Lord of my Burning Passions' and 'Keeping Watch'.

Gopi Warrier for 'Cricket at Lords' and 'R.E.M.', both published in Gopi Warrier's *Lament of JC* (The Delhi London Poetry Foundation).

Eileen Wright for 'They Were Ready' and 'Voices', both published in *The Northern Durbar* (Pontefract Press & Kala Sangam), and 'The Earrings'.

The editor has made every effort to contact copyright holders and to obtain permissions prior to publication.